ROAD.IE, inc.!

How to Gain and Keep a Career in the Live Music Business
2nd Edition

Andy Reynolds

Acknowledgments

My thanks and love goes out to:

Lily Nelson

Mum, Jeremy, Sara, and Katie.

The Gleesons – Pat, Mike, Brian, Mary, Maggy, Kate, Celia, Annie and all their families.

Tracey, Ruby, and Megan Nelson.

All the crew I have had the honour to work with over the years, especially:

Noel Kilbride, Nick Jevons, Andy Dimmack, Ricky Ricketts, Tim Hardstaff, Paul Myers, Rich Bell, Jock Bain (RIP), Sean Gerrard, Chris Taplin, Mark Parsons, Anthony Oates, Timm Cleasby, Nigel Reeks and The DCL "Top Gun."

Everyone who consented to be interviewed. I hope I have used your words of wisdom in the best way.

The many bands and artists, booking agents, promoters, and artist managers who have put up with my eccentric style of tour management., - 'There has been a

terrible mistake."

Emily Wilson for the copy-editing help

Eileen for the unconditional love and support.

About the Author

Andy Reynolds has worked as an international concert tour manager and audio engineer for over 25 years. He has toured continuously during this time, working on an average of 200 shows per year. Andy has worked for such bands as The Pierces, Maverick Sabre, All-American Rejects, House of Pain, Machine Head, Nightmares On Wax, Pavement, Roots Manuva, Super Furry Animals, Skunk Anansie, Squarepusher, and The White Stripes. He has worked with bands on tours by such acts as U2, Whitney Houston, Manic Street Preachers, and Foo Fighters. His touring experience encompasses stadiums, arenas, theatres, pubs, bars, clubs, outdoor festivals, rooftops, subway stations, cruise ships, mountainsides, and very, very muddy fields.

Andy is the author of '*The Tour Book – How to get Your Music on the Road*', the musicians definitive guide to gigging and touring.

Andy has taught live sound engineering and concert tour management at

Buckinghamshire New University, Liverpool University, Red Tape Studios (Sheffield) and City College Manchester., and conducted seminars for such bodies as the Audio Engineering Society.

Learn more about Andy at www.livemusicbusiness.com

ISBN-13: 978-1456549688

ISBN-10: 1456549685

Printed in the United States of America

Contents

Acknowledgments   3

About the Author   4

The Live Music Business Today

So you want to work in the live music business?   13

Be prepared - get the answers   15

Who Does What?

The Management   18

The Agent   27

The Promoter   36

The Promoter's Representative   47

The Crew   50

Touring/Visiting Crew   57

How do you join these people on-the-road?   66

Why live music industry jobs are never advertised   67

Live music business jobs are different   68

Why you need to treat your career as a business   71

Set up your own

freelance crew business

Planning your freelance business   72

Sections of your business plan   73

Which business 'type' to choose   75

Help and advisors   75

Financing your business   77

Timing   81

Get to know local talent.   85

Getting started

Build up your network.   89

Use your network   90

Training   94

Courses and qualifications   95

Books, magazines and websites   99

Broaden your skills.   100

Get that experience.   103

Selling your services   111

Getting hired

Initial interest. (a.k.a. advertising)   112

Web sites   113

Fig 5.01 The Complete FOH Engineer Page on Facebook   117

Social media   117

'Brochures'   118

Résumés   120

Working on recommendation   125

Getting those recommendations   127

Payment and invoicing   133

How do you keep

working in the live music business?

Check your client.   135

Get a contract   136

Pay rates   145

Plan ahead   147

Health and conditions   148

Conclusion

Appendix 1

Specific job roles, skills and qualifications   153

Artist management   154

Booking agent   156

Concert promoter   158

Promoter's rep   160

Tour manager   162

Production manager   164

Audio crew – systems tech   166

Audio crew – band   168

Lighting crew – systems tech   170

Lighting crew – Lighting Designer/operator   172

Video crew   174

Backline crew   176

Rigger   178

Caterer   180

Stagehand   182

Driver   184

Tour security   186

Merchandiser   187

Tour accountant   189

Stylist - Wardrobe   190

Appendix 2

Quotes from live music business professionals.   191

Getting started: 191

How do you choose your Tour Managers and touring crew?

    192

References

1 The Live Music Business Today

You obviously have an interest in the music business and so could not have failed to notice the fantastic changes taking place in the industry. Every other day there seems to be a newspaper or magazine article reporting that CD sales are falling, record companies are in financial free-fall and that artists are relying on their concerts to make them money. The Sunday Times went so far as declaring October 7th 2007 as "the day the music industry died", citing "There is no money in recorded music any more, that's why bands are now giving it away [1]."

In fact bands are not giving away their music entirely for free. Live music is very much in demand by music fans and although recorded music may be 'given away' and used as a loss-leader, every band and artist should be aware of the potential financial benefit of concerts and touring. The numbers speak for themselves: 65 million people attended a live music show in 2010; total gross for those shows was $3.3 billion [2]. A Rolling Stone magazine survey of the richest musicians noted "The vast majority of artists in our Top Thirty made the bulk of their cash on the road. Album royalties pale in comparison." [3]. U2 were the richest in 2010, netting $130 million as a result of their 'U2 360°' tour, despite disappointing sales of their last album. "In today's world artists have to tour to make money. They can't just sit at home and collect their royalties and expect to make their mortgage payments," says Gary Bongiovanni, editor of Pollstar, a music business magazine. [4]

On a smaller scale, independent artists such as Amanda Palmer, Imogen Heap and Gov't Mule make much of their income from performing live. Gov't Mule tour regularly and since 2004 have grossed more than $600,000 per year alone from recordings of their shows that fans can download direct from the 'Mule Tracks' website (figure 1.01).

Figure 1.01. Gov't Mule's ecommerce site.

It is not just a question of cash. The perceived increase in the importance of concerts and touring for artists has had a massive effect on the nature of the music business in general. Live Nation, the concert promoters who did not even exist 8 years ago, have signed U2, Nickelback, Shakira, Jay-Z and Madonna to '360 degree' deals that see the artists and Live Nation share revenue not only from concerts and touring but from the recordings and artist merchandise. In signing these artists Live Nation has directly challenged (and acquired artists from) the established recorded music giants such as EMI, Universal and Sony.

There are other examples of the continuing dominance of live music. I have worked with unsigned and independent bands who sell out 1000 capacity venues, spreading the word on the back of solid touring and online activity and all without the backing of a record company or even any physical record sales. Young bands, signed or not, are touring from the beginning of their careers, increasing numbers of venues are hosting live music and more people are directly employed in the live music industry.

These are obviously exciting times for anyone involved with live music. Are you going to be part of this fast growing industry?

So you want to work in the live music business?

You will see from the examples at the start of this chapter that there is enormous potential to find yourself an exciting and financially rewarding career in live music. The industry is growing and with that growth there is increasing structure and stability. Yet, compared with recorded music or retail, the live industry is comparatively small. And like most niche industries, that means it is hard to break into, find work and establish yourself.

In my work as a band tour manager I receive numerous enquiries from people wanting insider hints and tips on how to get jobs and a career in the live music industry, usually along the lines of, "I wanna be a roadie; take me on tour." This worries me slightly because obviously the image of "roadies" in most people's minds is of a group of people so unskilled that anyone can suddenly become one (figure 1.02).

Figure 1.02. Roadies – it's not just a matter of dressing in black and hanging around with rock stars.

These emails, letters and phone calls also share the same frustration that there seems to be no recognised career path and little or no qualified information on how to gain and keep work in the live music business. The overall feeling from people not currently engaged in the industry is that the barriers to entry are immense and, once you have made the entry into the industry, you face even more hard work. I agree. And, at the same time, I have witnessed so many crew really mess it up for themselves by being unprepared, unprofessional or ignorant about the industry they work in.

It always strikes me as being a shame when touring crew act this way – surely this is the dream they have been working towards? Why throw away the chances of a lifetime by being unprepared?

You are doing the right thing though – by reading this book you are going to learn how to be prepared.

Be prepared - get the answers

Being on-the-road is not a case of simply hanging around with pop bands; to be effective and to keep your job you need to be skilled, professional, selfless and compassionate. You are going to be dealing with insecure and worried artists, artists who are sometimes completely out of their depth in the concert environment. You cannot be seen to panic when things go wrong. You are paid to make sure things go right every time the band sets foot on a stage. You will be part of a large professional team, working independently and with limited access to the band members. You will definitely have very little opportunity for socialising with the band or hanging around in glamorous situations.

It is true that years ago bands would employ a general "roadie" who would shift cases, set up gear, and generally take care of everything to do with the stage. Today, this role is still applicable to some bands, especially in the early days of their career. This kind of road crew person does have a lot of contact with the band they work for and they will get seen with the band, on stage and at social events. I suppose the image of this kind of familiarity excites potential road crew people. They see the 'roadies' having direct contact with the band, living on the same tour bus and staying in the same hotels, even the same hotel rooms, as band members. The life looks glamorous and makes potential entrants into the industry excited. This excitement is misguided; today's live production industry is made up of highly specialised touring professionals. (figure 1.03).

Let's go and meet them.

Figure 1.03. Road crew are experienced and dedicated professionals.

2 Who Does What?

Whether you are starting out or you consider yourself to be highly experienced, it is always useful to know the components of your business. I have met many successful musicians who still do not know the difference between promoters and booking agents, for example. (Do not worry if you do not know the difference, you are about to find out in this chapter.) I remember working on my first professional tours and the assumptions and mistakes I made about the tour organisers, promoters, and various crew I met. Although the relative roles in the professional setting may seem irrelevant to you now, it is vitally important that you understand how a show is put together and who does what and why. After all, you are going to be working with all these people one day.

In this section I will outline briefly each person's role in the planning, booking, or running of a show (figure 2.01). Remember you only have one chance when applying for a crew job. A little research now will prevent embarrassing mistakes later. Make sure you know who you are talking to and you understand their responsibilities.

Figure 2.01. This is what the touring crew work towards – the band on stage and the crowd going wild.

The Management

Although managers are not 100-percent involved in the day-to-day mechanics of a show or event, I have included information here because, as a performer or behind-the-scenes person, you will invariably run into managers as your first point of contact. Trying to get an opening slot on a show, applying for a touring job, trying to arrange an artist interview or book a show—in all these cases, you will need the permission of the management.

The artist manager (also known as the personal manager in the U.S.) is the spoke around which the wheel of the artist's career should revolve. The manager's job is to represent the artist in all business areas and to guide him or her toward the best logistical and financial decisions. Obviously this role extends to recordings, publishing, and non-performance promotional activities, but it is the role of the artist manager in shows and touring that is relevant here.

I'm not going to waffle on about artist managers too much— for more detailed information about how to find and work with a manager, you should read the very excellent '*All You Need To Know About The Music Business*', (Simon & Schuster, 2006) by Donald S. Passman. At this point you do need to know that an artist will approach or be approached by a manager who agrees to handle his or her affairs for a percentage of the artist's gross earnings (usually between 10 and 20 percent, with most managers taking 15 percent). The manager and artist should sign a contract to stipulate this arrangement or at very least sign an agreement stating the intentions of each party over a given time period, say six months or a year. (Generally, "make me rich and famous by next week" is not a suitable artist/manager agreement).

Although not strictly involved in the booking of a show or tour, the managers to whom I spoke were unanimous in their support for playing live. "It's fundamental that a band plays live, especially in the current climate," says Ben Kirby, manager of the Subways (figure 2.02). "There's such a fast turnover of acts these days, and it's vital to gig your arse off and build a solid fan base that will still be there in five years and will see you through any downturns [5]."

Figure 2.02. Charlotte Cooper of The Subways, a band who built a solid fan base through constant touring.

A good manager should therefore be looking to make sure the act he or she represents is capable and ready to play live, both to perhaps score a record deal and, more importantly, to gain a strong audience fan base.

Because touring can be expensive, the band you work for will need a manager who can raise finances and keep good track of expenses. As well as handling finances and publicity and organizing and overseeing rehearsals, the manager can either find work for the artist himself or find and use a booking agent. In the early days, most managers will have to book shows for their artists themselves; after a degree of success (or a label signing), the artist management will likely work with a booking agent.

Remember, the manager's job is to secure the most lucrative and wide-reaching activities for his or her act; simply advising the team to "go out and get loads of shows" is not good business sense (even thought it will benefit you as touring crew). The artist manager has to present logistical and financial information to the booking agent in order for the agent to work effectively. Performing shows or touring should complement any other activities in which the artist is involved, and good lines of communication should exist between the artist manager, the booking agent, the record company, the publicity departments, and the tour crew.

Once the manager is presented with a list of potential concert dates by the booking agent, it is his or her job to make sure the tour or show is viable for the artist. The manager will work out a budget or employ a tour manager (hey, that's me!) to work out a budget for her. The booking agent will have given the manager a list of the fees (income from ticket sales) the band will receive on the tour. The person responsible for the budget should then subtract cost figures for the following likely expenses:

- Wages

- Per diems

- Accommodations

- Transportation

- Sound

- Lighting

- Video

- Production—other items necessary to create the show

- Visas and work papers

- Rehearsals

- Agent's commission

- Management commission

- Foreign Artist tax

The show/tour income minus the expenses listed will give either the profit or loss figure for the tour. A loss is called a shortfall. (Figure 2.03.)

REVISION:	MILLIONS OF AMERICANS US TOUR - SPRING 2007		Days= 11 Shows= 7	
	EXPENSES SUMMARY		TOTAL COST	
TOTAL EXPENSES	WAGES		$13,860.00	
	PER DIEMS		$1,035.00	
	ACCOMMODATION		$2,055.00	
	TRANSPORT		$18,797.56	
	SOUND		$0.00	
	LIGHTS		$3,520.00	
	VIDEO		$0.00	
	BACKLINE		$2,730.00	
	SET & STAGE		$0.00	
	PRODUCTION		$4,160.00	
	REHEARSALS		$1,720.00	
	OTHER EXPENSE		$2,240.00	
		TOTAL	$50,117.56	
INCOME	7 shows at $3200	$3,200.00 7	$22,400.00	
		INCOME TOTAL	$22,400.00	
PROFIT / LOSS	EXPENSES		$50,117.56	
	5% CONTINGENCY		$2,505.88	
	PROFIT/LOSS		**-$30,223.43**	

Figure 2.03. The summary page of a typical tour expenses sheet.

Once a budget has been worked out to the manager's approval, a couple of things may happen. If the budget shows a profit or if the band is not beholden to any record label or other financial concern (in other words, if they are as big as U2, Deadmau5 or the Foo Fighters), then the manager will approve the tour and tell the agent to go ahead and confirm the shows. The tour is then on.

If the budget shows a loss/shortfall, then the band can either cancel the proposed tour or try to find extra income from somewhere. The most common route (if applicable) is to go to the record label and ask for tour support. Tour support is money advanced to the act by the label to enable the act to go off and tour. The thinking is that the touring will help to promote the act and sell more records, so record companies see a benefit and will grant tour support. Obtaining a decent amount of tour support is difficult these days because the fortunes of the record companies have suffered setbacks recently. (One enterprising manager once described record company advances in general and particularly tour support as a "big, fat interest-free loan." While the analogy makes the process easy to explain, I would certainly seek proper legal advice if entering into a recording contract.)

If you were in a band and applying for tour support, the record company accountants would want to see a copy of the proposed budget. The budget will be scrutinized and objections will be made regarding any unauthorized or unnecessary expenses. Even though the tour support is recoupable from the artist and is basically a loan, record companies have very clear guidelines about what they will and will not fund when supplying tour support. For instance, Universal Music Group (UMG) have produced a 'handbook' to help artist managers, tour managers and the acts themselves understand how UMG allocates tour support to its touring acts. The introduction to this handbook reads:

> "As we are all aware, live work can be a key tool in helping to break an artist. Tour support exists to help make up the difference between costs and income. As we all know the early stages of an artist's live career are rarely profitable. The main principal underpinning the evaluation of a request for tour support is a simple question: Is the shortfall a good investment for both the

artist and the label?

To answer this question many issues have to be considered. Examples of these might include: Does the artist have records to promote in that particular territory? Is the tour relevant to where the artist is currently positioned in the market? Other factors might include venue size, other artists on the bill, location of venues, timing of the tour and likely sales and promotional benefits that will arise." [6]

The manager's responsibility to his or her artist therefore is to ensure the budget/list of expenses for the tour is reasonable and bona fide. Once the label's accountant is satisfied, he will approve the budget and arrange for the amount of the shortfall to be paid to the band. The manager then makes a final decision and if he or she feels the tour is viable, the manager will inform the agent to confirm the gigs. The tour is on (again).

Note: How Tour Support Is Paid. You just want to work for bands on-the-road, why do you need to know all this? Well, the payment of tour support has a direct impact on your salary, so read on. A band will usually need to apply to their record company for tour support, each and every time they want to go on tour. If that application is approved, the record company will usually stagger the payment of the tour support. They do not just hand over $50,000 and let them climb into the back of a 15-seat passenger van and head off on tour. A typical scenario for payment of tour support is a 75/25 ratio, where 75 percent of the shortfall is paid before the start of the tour and the remaining 25 percent is payable on receipt of the tour accounts at the end of the tour. This is important to you because your wages will probably be paid out of the 25% chunk that arrives when the accounts are complete. If there is a problem or delay with reconciling those accounts then the band will not be able to pay you. You will have worked for a month and then may have to wait for another month to get paid.

The manager is also responsible for overseeing the expenses incurred on the road—even if he or she has employed a tour manager. The tour manager should have responsibility for expenditures in line with the agreed budget, but if there is an emergency or if an unpredicted expense arises, the tour manager should definitely seek the manager's approval before spending any more money. At the end of the day the manager has to justify the expenses and any budget overrun to the label accountant. If the label feels the expenses are over and above what was agreed upon, they can withhold the remaining shortfall or deduct unwarranted expenses from the due amount. The effect of this could bankrupt a band. A manager therefore has to have a firm grip on touring expenses.

There is a (probably) apocryphal story that illustrates this point. A UK band touring the US became so miserable on the road that they demanded the tour manager arrange hotel rooms for them each night, in addition to the very expensive sleeper bus they were already using. This was obviously not an approved expense and it caused the shortfall to expand considerably. In desperation the artist manager applied to the label for more tour support. The label agreed, but used money allocated for recording the next album to fund this extra tour support. All tour expenses were paid in full, but the following album had to be recorded on a much tighter budget. Whether or not it is true, the story illustrates just how careful a manager has to be in keeping touring costs in check. As the Universal Music Group handbook on tour support says, "We will want anyone working for our artists to agree to policies on hotels, P.D's, travel and other matters". [6]

The Agent

A talent agent is someone who finds paid engagements (film, TV, radio writing) for creative people. A talent agent who finds gigs, shows and tours for a band or singer is known as a booking agent; the process of securing a show or tour is known as a booking – hence the name. The booking agent does not actually arrange to put on shows; they simply represent the artist to promoters who may want to put on a show featuring that artist.

Booking agents are usually larger agencies comprised of a number of individual agents. The agents are responsible for their own revenues and use the agency's infrastructure (including telephone, internet, and legal and accountancy services) to help run their own "micro-business" within the overall framework of the agency. The agency then takes a cut of the agent's revenue to pay for these services and to (hopefully) generate a profit. This type of agent represents professional acts that usually have a recording contract. The agent works closely with the manager and also the record labels to coordinate a promotional schedule based on concert touring. Major agencies include Creative Artists Agency, William Morris Endeavor, Artists Group International, Little Big Man Booking, the Agency Group, and X-Ray Touring.

Some smaller booking agents will run a stable of similar acts, such as DJs, tribute bands, presenters, or blues acts. They provide a service to these acts by supplying them to venues and markets demanding that type of act. In general, they represent semi-professional or niche artists.

An agent makes money by charging their client (the artist) a percentage of that artist's gross income for the performance. This commission is set at 10% in the US by regulation from the various entertainment unions – AFM (American Federation of Musicians, AFTRA (American Federation of Television and Radio Artists) and SAG (Screen Actors Guild). There is no official regulation in the UK concerning agency commission but 10% seems to be the norm [7].

If an agent makes a deal with a promoter that sees the promoter providing non-cash additions, such as hotels or executive transportation, then the agent will often calculate the cash equivalent of these "special terms and conditions" and charge a percentage of the perceived value of these items when calculating the commission due. After all, the agent did negotiate very strenuously on behalf of the artist to secure these non-cash perks; it is therefore only fair that the agent should be compensated further. It is thus very important that the artist manager has access to a highly experienced accountant who can verify the true cash worth of these intangibles. What percentage of the Sony PlayStation included backstage should a booking agent charge for?

The agent should have a rough idea of the logistical and financial expectations his or her artists will have for performing live. This information can be summarized in the contract and contract rider information that will legally bind any booking made by the agent (figures 2.04 & 2.07).

Having agreed upon a period of touring or concert activity with the artist's manager, the agent will approach promoters and offer the artists services. The agent will attempt to secure a guaranteed fee (the front end) for the performance as well as some kind of bonus percentage if the show sells a lot of tickets (the back end). It is the agent's job to negotiate the deals with the promoter based on what he or she knows of the act's status, the city or venue he or she is pitching to, and the relationship with the promoter. It is no good trying to get a $1,000 fee for a newly signed act in a bar in Spokane on a Sunday night, regardless of how much record-company backing and rock magazine covers you are getting. All good agents will have developed working relationships with the promoters to the extent that most of the negotiating is unsaid; each knows the other's business well.

This relationship also means that managers can rely on superstar agents to help break their acts. Agents such as Marty Diamond (the US agent for Coldplay, Snow Patrol, KT Tunstall, and Artic Monkeys) would obviously be more able to persuade a promoter to take on one of his small, unknown acts. The understanding would be that if the promoter works with this act now, then the agent will offer the promoter the chance to book a bigger act in the future. You will therefore find it extremely unlikely for a young act to be taken on by an agent at the very start of their career, as they will have to build up a certain amount of fans.

When an agreement has been reached between the agent and the promoter the agent will issue a contract on behalf of the band to the promoter. An example contract is shown in figure 2.04.

When booking shows, the agent has to take into account geographical and seasonal matters, as well as keep an eye on the competition. An agent will try to plan the routing of the tour when pitching to promoters. In practice, promoters will be offered their pick of dates depending on the location of the venue they are booking. For instance, in North America the agent will approach all promoters based in the Northwest (Portland, Seattle, Vancouver) with available dates in the first four days of the tour. Then he or she will approach promoters in California (San Francisco, Los Angeles, San Diego, and so on) with possible openings for the following four or five days. In the UK it would be openings in Scotland for the first couple of days, and then maybe promoters in Liverpool, Manchester, and Carlisle would be approached for the next week of the tour.

Hopefully, the agent can then present a fairly logical routing for the tour, such as north to south or clockwise around the country. This will ensure less travelling and cheaper transportation costs.

This type of planning has to be done well in advance (typically three to four months) to ensure availability in the regions wanted. Sometimes it is just not possible, and you end up with the much-dreaded "Star of David" tour in which every show seems to be at the geographical opposite from the previous performance.

Seasonal matters also come into play. It is pointless to try to book a club tour of Europe between June and August if you represent an indie/alternative act. The vast majority of music fans will be headed for one of the many festivals, such as Coachella, Benicassim, Reading & Leeds (figure 2.05), Pukkelpop, and Roskilde. These music fans will also include your smaller club promoters! Likewise, a coast-to-coast tour of Canada in January/February would be pretty pointless. Even if you could make it through the snow, would the audience turn up?

Contract No.: **1234**

An Agreement made the 01st day of January 2013

Between **P. Romoter pp TKN Concerts, 123 Gig Street**, London hereinafter referred to as the 'Promoter' of the one part

AND **Ron Decline pp Millions of Americans** hereinafter referred to as the 'Artiste' of the other part.

WITNESSETH that the Promoter hereby engages the Artiste and the Artiste agrees to the engagement to appear/perform as **Millions of Americans** at the venues(s), on the dates and for the periods and at the salary stated hereto.

SCHEDULE

The Artiste agrees to appear at ONE (1) performance as follows:

At the: **Fleapit**
                                             1 Deedah Street
                                             Sheffield

                                             S1

On the: **Saturday, 25th April 2013**

Capacity: **350**

Ticket price: **$6.00 in advance**

For a salary of: **$300.00 plus PA/lights + catering**
or 80% of door receipts (after $1116.43 costs) whichever is the greater

---

SPECIAL STIPULATIONS

1)   The exact running times for this engagement are to be advised.

Signed_____Date_____

This agency is not responsible for any non-fulfilment of contracts by Proprietors, Managers or Artists but every reasonable safeguard is assured.

Contract No.: **1234 continued**

2) Payment

The guaranteed fee for this engagement is $300.00 + 80% of door receipts, after costs, which is payable to the Artiste as follows:

a) A deposit of 50% of the fee, i.e. $150.00, is payable to by certified check to TKN CONCERTS CLIENTS ACCOUNT and should be posted to TKN Concerts, 123 Gig Street London. **Deposit due immediately on receipt of contract**. In the event of cancellation by the Promoter, this will be retained by the Artiste.

For the purposes of this clause time is of the essence.

b) The balance of the fee, i.e. $150.00, plus any percentage payments due, is payable to the Artiste in cash pounds Sterling on the night of the performance.

c) The fee should be net and free of all local taxation.

3) Sound and Lights.

Promoter is to provide and pay for a first class P.A. and Monitor system and Lighting systems to the Artistes specification and approval (see attached technical specifications). All the necessary crew is to be in attendance throughout sound check and for the duration of Artistes entire performance.

4) Sponsorship and Endorsement.

The name or logo of Millions of Americans or any of its members shall not be used by any sponsor or be tied to any commercial product or company, nor there be any sign, banner or advertising at or within 30 meters of the stage throughout the entire engagement. Promoter is specifically prohibited from associating Artistes name with any product or sponsorship or promotion whatsoever without Artistes prior approval and written consent.

5) Merchandising.

The Artiste shall have the exclusive right but not obligation to sell souvenirs, posters, programs, shirts and all other merchandise directly pertaining to and/or bearing the likeness of the Artistes at the engagement and to retain ALL monies received from the sale thereof.

Promoter shall ensure that there is sufficient space for suitable stands to be erected for this purpose at no cost to Artiste.

6) Unauthorized recording.

a) The Promoter agrees that no part of the performance may be taped, filmed or otherwise recorded in any way whatsoever. Promoter shall place a sign at the entrance(s) to the engagement which clearly states this limitation.

b) Promoter shall ensure that no recordings take place and shall confiscate or otherwise detain any sound or visual recording materials by visually screening all persons attending the engagement for any recording equipment. Promoter agrees to cooperate fully with Artistes to prevent such recordings and agree to act promptly and diligently

Contract No.: **1234 continued**

to all Artistes requests in fulfilment of this clause.

c) It is agreed and understood that in no instance whatsoever will the Artistes allow filming recording or broadcasts of any type at the aforementioned venue (by persons known or unknown) including but not limited to TV, film, radio, video tape and digital media unless the Artiste gives their prior written consent.

7) Decline to perform

The Artiste reserves the right to decline to perform without prejudice to the full agreed fee in the event of any reason beyond the control of the Artiste including but not limited to strike, lock out, war, fire, serious or dangerous weather conditions.

Signed_____Date_____

Figure 2.04. A standard performance contract between the agent and the promoter.

Finally, both agents and promoters should have a keen eye on international sports fixtures. These events are direct competition to music events and, unfortunately, music always loses.

When the agent has provisionally booked the act into various cities, he or she will inform the artist manager of the dates on offer and the fees expected. If the manager and label (as discussed earlier) approve the tour, the agent will issue contracts to the promoters. The agent will then be available to answer any further questions or concerns the manager or promoters may have before the tour and will act as a go-between should any disagreements arise during the tour itself.

I have no doubt that booking agents are the most powerful people in today's live music business and you are well advised to make friends with as many agents as you can in order to gain and keep work in the touring industry.

Figure 2.05. Main Stage, Reading Festival, England.

The Promoter

In the UK and Europe, these people are known as promoters; in the US they are known as talent buyers. Whatever the terminology may be, these are the brave souls who decide they can make money out of putting on a show or event. (The term promoter is because they promote an event to make money; talent buyer is because they er, buy the, er...talent that will, er...sell tickets. You get the idea.)

The promoter's goal is simple - put bums/asses on seats. They take an event, put it into a suitable venue, and sell tickets to the public. Some venues manage their promotions (in-house), but usually venues are hired by a promoter to stage the show. There is an enormous risk involved with promotion, but a good promoter will look at turning a profit over the long term by developing good relationships with the booking agents. A good relationship with the agents means direct access to the agent's roster and his or her more successful acts.

Most promoting today is done by companies that (like booking agencies) consist of a number of individual promoters. As we have seen, there is a lot of money to be made from concerts. The last 20 years have seen the creation of several huge concert-promoting companies. The major player in the US is Live Nation (figure 2.06) who promoted 21,700 events in 2011, grossing $6.5 billion [8]. AEG LIVE Outback Concerts and Paragon are also doing well. In the UK, Live Nation and AEG are again very strong, along with Festival Republic, SJM, DF Concerts and Metropolis Music Group.

So how does it all work? Well, promoters are approached by an agent, manager, or artist to stage a show, or (very importantly) they scout around for good moneymaking opportunities. The recent success of re-formed bands from the 1970s and 1980s is due in no small part to promoters seeing the financial potential. Mags Revell, a promoter at Metropolis Music Group, worked hard to persuade the original members of Motley Crüe to re-form for a concert tour. After a gap of nearly seven years and with no record to promote, the band hit the road in 2005, playing in 60 cities and grossing $40 million in North America alone.

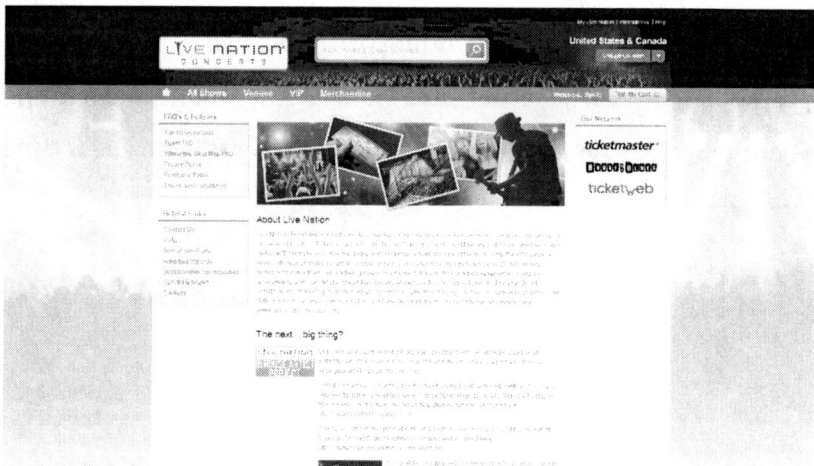

Figure 2.06. Live Nation, complete with Live Nation Artists, are the predominant force in concert promoting.

Whether the attraction is a superstar act, such as Motley Crüe, or an unknown and unproven act the principle is the same: The promoter will examine the costs involved in staging the event and the profit potential to him and to the act. He will then propose a financial offer to the act that will incorporate what he knows about the act's technical production requirements. At this point the promoter will probably not have a full contract and rider from the agent, but he can make an educated guess about what he is going to offer based on similar acts and his experience. (An example rider is shown in figure 2.07.)

The promoter is then responsible for advertising the show and selling the tickets. If he doesn't advertise and sell tickets, he isn't going to make any money. He will work with the act's record company, PR, and plugging firms to ensure maximum publicity for the event. Additionally, and depending on the act's contract terms, the promoter may also be responsible for arranging sound and lighting equipment, transportation, accommodations, and catering for the band and its crew.

MILLIONS OF AMERICANS EUROPE 2013

THIS RIDER FORMS AN INTEGRAL PART OF THE CONTRACT (#1234) TO WHICH IT IS ANNEXED.

CAST & CREW

Millions of Americans are 9 people:

4 x band

1 x TM/FOH engineer Andy Reynolds

Contact: T: +44 (0)7762 551886   E: andy.reynolds@tourconcepts.com

1 x Driver D. River

Contact: T: +44 (0)7777 12345   E: sprinter@merc.com

1 x back line technician C. Himp

Contact: T: +44 (0)7777 98765   E: chimp@hotmail.com

1 x lighting engineerMs. L. Ampy

Contact: T: +44 (0)7777 90909   pulsarrules@aol.com

1 x merchandise seller S. Wag

Contact: T: +44 (0)7777 00700   isithereyet@yahoo.co.uk

Millions of Americans are NOT travelling with a monitor engineer. The purchaser agrees to supply one sound engineer(s) who is capable and willing of mixing monitor sound for Millions of Americans, at no cost to the artist.

Cast and crew will travel together in one (1) vehicle as listed below. This vehicle also contains all the backline and lighting equipment.

PREPARED BY ANDY REYNOLDS - TOUR MANAGER
T: +44 (0) 7762 551886 T: +44 (0)870 126 5960
Email: andy.reynolds@tourconcepts.com

THIS RIDER EXPIRES AUGUST 30th 2013

PAGE 1 of 6

1. ACCESS AND EQUIPMENT

The Purchaser agrees to provide and pay for 2 (TWO) able bodied and sober persons to assist the Artiste with the get in and get out of the Artistes equipment. The Purchaser also agrees to provide 1 (ONE) runner with own reliable transport.

The Purchaser agrees to allow access to the venue/ performance space at a reasonable time as specified and agreed by the Artistes Tour Manager. Artiste reserves the right to supplement certain sound and lighting equipment after consultation with the Purchaser; in such cases the Purchaser will provide and pay for a fully qualified electrician and provide and pay for all necessary sound and lighting operatives necessary to assist in installation of supplementary sound and lighting equipment.

2. PA and LIGHTS

See separate technical rider for Artistes specific requirements.

Millions of Americans are carrying their own In Ear Monitor system (IEM). This operates on 832.700 MHz (EBU CH 66) and be altered between 830 to 866 MHz. For full details please see attached technical specifications and/or contact Andy Reynolds on +44 (0)551886 or email andy.reynolds@tourconcepts.com

Millions of Americans are carrying their own lighting system which will complement the existing venue lighting system. For full details please see attached technical specifications and/or contact Ms. L. Ampy on +44 (0)7777 90909 or email pulsarrules@aol.com

3. PARKING

The purchaser agrees to ensure parking space for:

1x Mercedes Vario band splitter van VRN # STA 456

This parking space should be adjacent to venue load in and be secure and free of cost to the Artiste.

4. MERCHANDISING

The Purchaser agrees to allow the Artiste sole right to erect stands for the sale of merchandise, in a clean and well lit area, at no charge whatsoever to the Artiste.

PREPARED BY ANDY REYNOLDS - TOUR MANAGER
T: +44 (0) 7762 551886 T: +44 (0)870 126 5960
Email: andy.reynolds@tourconcepts.com

THIS RIDER EXPIRES AUGUST 30th 2013

5. GUEST LIST

The Artiste reserves the right to admit up to 25 guests free of charge and this will not prejudice the Artistes fee. Purchaser agrees to confirm numbers of Purchasers own guests with Artiste's Tour Manager before opening the venue to the public.

6. SETTLEMENT

The Purchaser agrees to provide all documentation relating to the Artiste's performance for the inspection by Artiste and Artiste's Tour Manager. This documentation including but not limited to pre - sale ticket reports, show cost receipts, on night ticket sale reports and tax exemption submissions should be available at time of settlement, usually one hour before completion of Artiste's performance. The Purchaser agrees that all relevant show costs should have corresponding receipts and that failure to provide original receipts will result in corresponding cost to be null and void.

7. SECURITY

Purchaser agrees to provide and pay for adequate numbers of reliable and reputable security personnel with clearly marked apparel and identification. Such personnel should report to designated security manager who in turn follows instruction from Artiste's Tour Manager. Purchaser agrees to coordinate with security manager and Artiste Tour Manager regarding particular security arrangements, in particular pit crew etiquette and instruction.

The Purchaser shall guarantee proper security at all times to ensure the safety of the Artiste, auxiliary personal, instruments and all equipment, costumes, vehicles and personal property during and after the performance. Particular security must be provided in the areas of the stage, dressing room and all exits and entrances to the auditorium, mixing consoles and Artiste merchandising stalls.

Security protection is to commence upon arrival of the Artiste on the premises, until equipment is re-packed into transportation and Artiste personnel have left the premises.

Artiste will provide laminated passes that shall be sole accreditation valid on day of Artiste's performance. Artiste's Tour Manager will approve and issue sticky passes for all non- - touring personnel. The Artiste reserves the right to refuse any accreditation issued by Purchaser or venue.

PREPARED BY ANDY REYNOLDS - TOUR MANAGER
T: +44 (0) 7762 551886 T: +44 (0)870 126 5960
Email: andy.reynolds@tourconcepts.com

THIS RIDER EXPIRES AUGUST 30th 2013
PAGE 3 of 6

8. SUPPORT/ OPENING ACTS

The Artiste reserves the right to approve and or amend support/-opening acts. The Purchaser agrees not to add other acts other than those approved by the Artiste in writing.

The Artiste reserves the right to dictate the running order of the show and the acts appearing therein. The Artiste reserves the right to advise or amend any music, film or performance relating to the Artiste's performance including but not limited to intro music, play on music, after show DJ's and video compilations.

9. CATERING AND HOSPITALITY

The Purchaser agrees to provide the following:

Clean and hygienic toilet and sanitary facilities, including 2 (two) showers with hot and cold water available all day, must be provided. If these are not available within the venue/ performance area, arrangements must be made at a local hotel (or other) facility.

Dressing Room (band)

This room must be clean, well lit, furnished and lockable and in a secure area. 220v outputs and sufficient furniture (including full-length) for a minimum of eight (8) people. Adequate climate control or heating control in winter months is essential.

2 x large trash/rubbish bins.

Twenty (20) large, clean towels with soap required from sound check time

Oil lamps, incense, candles, drapes and flowers are all welcome and should be included to improve the ambience of the environment.

Support band Dressing Room (TBC)

As above (see separate rider for catering/towels etc)

Production office

A secure production office that can be locked with telephone, desk, chair, Ethernet/ CAT 5 cabling, and/ or Wi-fi connection. (please supply access codes, network keys etc), RJ111 phone sockets and 220v power will be required wherever possible. Please provide the production Tel/fax numbers ASAP in advance.

PREPARED BY ANDY REYNOLDS - TOUR MANAGER
T: +44 (0) 7762 551886 T: +44 (0)870 126 5960
Email: andy.reynolds@tourconcepts.com

THIS RIDER EXPIRES AUGUST 30th 2013

PAGE 4 of 6

Crew Room

As band (no mirror required) – 10 (10) towels and soap at load in.

Catering

At load in time (13.00) for 5 people (crew plus driver(s)):

Constant hot tea & coffee set up (with biscuits etc)

Bottled still mineral water (Volvic, Spa or Evian)

Assorted Coca - Cola (no Pepsi!) Dr. Pepper etc

Assorted fruit juices (cranberry, orange, apple etc)

From 16.00 (4PM) band dressing room (drinks on ice):

8 x fresh vegetarian sandwiches (or sandwich ingredients plus bread)

24 x good quality local/imported bottled beer

20x I litre still mineral water (Volvic, Spa or Evian)

Assorted soft drinks, fresh OJ, apple juice, cranberry juice, Cokes etc

1 bottle of good quality local wine

1 x litre bottle quality vodka (Stoli, Findlandia, Moskosavoya etc NO ABSOLUT!)

Constant tea, coffee and hot water set up

Lemons and honey

Tissues, chocolates and chewing gum assortment

At 18.00 (6PM) main meal time for miniMom eight (8) people (including 2 vegetarians)

A covered dining table in a clean, smoke free and warm location (not the dressing room) with metal cutlery, appropriate crockery and condiments. Some band members may elect to eat after the show and this facility must be available. Drinks should be re-iced as required.

PREPARED BY ANDY REYNOLDS - TOUR MANAGER
T: +44 (0) 7762 551886 T: +44 (0)870 126 5960
Email: andy.reynolds@tourconcepts.com

THIS RIDER EXPIRES AUGUST 30th 2013

NOTE:

A hot, nutritious meal is always preferable. Should there be no alternative a buy-out of £10/€ 20 per person is acceptable. Please check with the Tour Manager in advance.

Food:

Individual place settings with assorted local breadbasket

Choice of starter (hot & cold) plus large fresh washed mixed salad bowl with dressings.

Hot choice of three entrees with vegetables, not limited to:

Vegetarian option (can include pasta)

White meat/ fish option

Red meat option

Sweet dessert course

Please leave some empty boxes in the dressing room to pack items at the end of the night

After show bus supplies:

Hot local take out speciality or pizza (1x vegetarian 1x other)

10 x sodas

PREPARED BY ANDY REYNOLDS - TOUR MANAGER
T: +44 (0) 7762 551886 T: +44 (0)870 126 5960
Email: andy.reynolds@tourconcepts.com

THIS RIDER EXPIRES AUGUST 30th 2013
PAGE 6 of 6

Figure 2.07. A contract rider. The contract is specific to a show; the rider contains information relevant to all the shows.

As I mentioned, promoting can be an enormously risky venture and possibly the most risky role out of the management/agent/promoter relationship. The fickleness of the concert-going public should never be underestimated. This uncertainty is the reason why specialized promotion companies, employing many individual promoters, handle most of the concert touring promotion these days. As production demands from the artists and tickets prices both increase, the potentially huge financial losses are too great for a one-man band or a small company. Recent years have therefore seen consolidation, buyouts, and mergers of talent buyers creating larger, more powerful promotions companies.

At this point I can hear you all saying, "Thanks for the business lesson, Andy, but what does that have to do with me?" I know you are impatient to get a job working in the live music industry. However, I did say you need to learn all the components to avoid making mistakes. A common mistake is to assume that the person who promotes the show is the same person you deal with over the phone and on the day. Let me explain.

All promoting companies, whether large or small, rely on new talent to create continual cash. Live Nation, SJM, AEG, and so on all need input from agents and the acts themselves as to what's hot and what's not. Promotion companies will employ two or three people who are the actual people constantly on the lookout for new talent, fielding calls from booking agents and working on the deals. These are the big girls and guys who make the calls, do the math, and sign the deal. Wham, deal is done, and then onto the next one. They do not have time to sort out sound and lights, print up dressing room signs, or arrange parking for 16 tour buses. Other people in the organization are employed for those roles, and it is very important that you, as crew person, do the research to find the right person to deal with.

For example, the majority of the bands that I tour with will do some UK shows that are promoted by SJM Concerts. (There are other promoters in the UK, such as Live Nation and Metropolis Music, to whom this example applies just as well.) Based in Manchester, SJM promote shows throughout England, ranging in size from 350-capacity club shows to stadium shows. Chris Yorke, as one of the heads of SJM, is responsible for doing the deals; therefore, every contract I receive for an SJM show bears his name. As tour manager, I am very unlikely to be in a position to question or change the deal the promoter has offered, and therefore I have very rarely spoken to Chris. What I need to sort out, as a tour manager, is load in, sound check and show times, bus parking, dressing room riders, PA and light specifications, curfew times, merchandising fees, and myriad other details. For this I speak to a very nice guy named Wayne Larner.

Wayne deals with the "production" of the show—the nuts and bolts. He has a huge database of every venue that SJM uses, so he can send me over information including stage sizes, power for buses, and whether the venue has stairs to the stage (very important!).

Wayne also receives information from Chris about the other acts playing on the show and how much is in the budget for catering. Wayne can therefore tell me what the show times will be and how many cans of cheap lager and supermarket sandwiches/deli trays he will give me for the "rider". I get all this information from Wayne for each SJM-promoted show on the tour and I make sure it fits in with what I am expecting and with what our contract stipulates. If challenges and issues arise, we try to come to a sensible arrangement, always bearing in mind that the financial deal for the show has already been done. If I start demanding extravagant sound equipment and tons of booze for backstage, based on the show deal already signed, the promoter will lose money. And because the promoter does not want to lose money, it is very unlikely that he or she will agree to my demands.

When I have all my information from Wayne (and the equivalent Waynes from the other promoters), I then set off on tour. On arriving at the first SJM show, I will see neither Chris nor Wayne. Chris is in the office doing deals, and Wayne is also in the office supplying advance information for future SJM shows. Chris and Wayne are not leaving me to fend for myself, though; they send down a representative.

The Promoter's Representative

The promoter's representative (or 'rep') is your point of contact for the promoter. Regardless of whether you are a performer, a tour manager, backline crew, or someone handing out flyers, if you want to speak to the promoter at a show, you will actually need to speak with the rep. The actual promoter will not be around until much later, if at all.

So the promoter is not at the show, and you have to deal with this rep. What can the rep do for you? Well, the rep's job is to be a liaison between the venue and the artist and to look out for the interests of the promoter. The rep will arrive at the same time as the main load in starts and is basically in charge of the show until the end of the night. The rep is there to ensure that the show goes smoothly, the band is paid correctly, the law is observed, and everything else in between goes well. Please do not assume I am talking about huge shows in theatres or arenas here. Remember, a successful promotions company may have 10 to 20 shows going on each night. Whether you are opening up in a 250-capacity bar or as a support DJ at a festival, you are going to be dealing with reps, not necessarily the person who has booked you for your show. The fact that you know a show is booked by a promoter but the day is handled by someone different should make your life a bit easier.

Figure 2.08 (overleaf). The people involved in putting on a show.

Venue

- Venue management
- Box office
- In-house promoter
- In-house techs

  - Audio
  - Lighting
  - Video

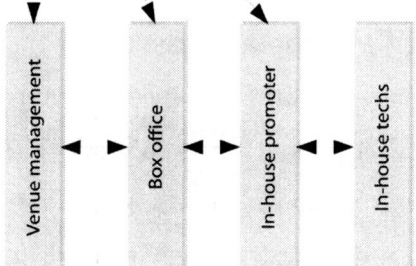

Outside promoter

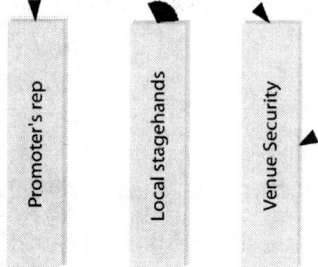

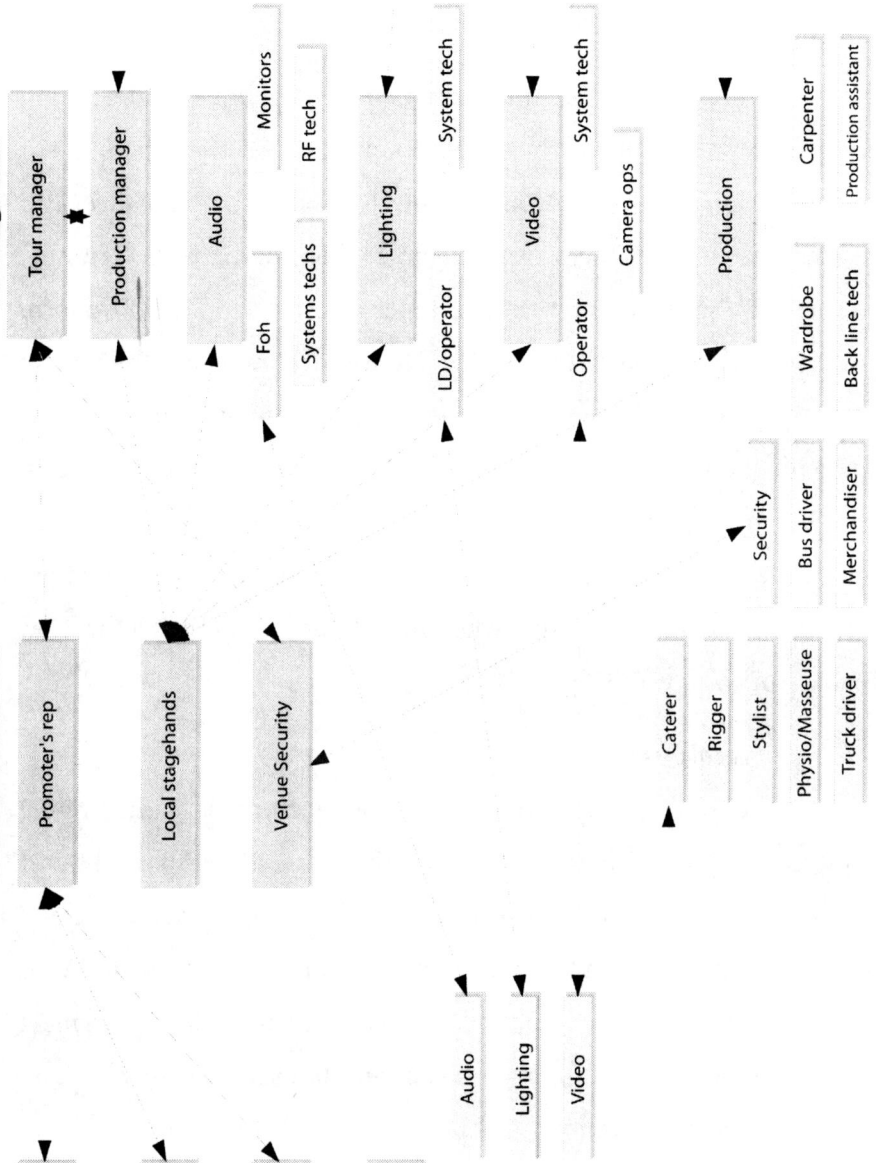

- Promoter's rep
- Local stagehands
- Venue Security

Touring crew

- Tour manager
- Production manager

  - Audio
    - Foh
    - Monitors
    - Systems techs
    - RF tech
  - Lighting
    - LD/operator
    - System tech
  - Video
    - Operator
    - System tech
    - Camera ops
  - Production
    - Security
    - Wardrobe
    - Carpenter
    - Bus driver
    - Back line tech
    - Production assistant
    - Merchandiser
    - Caterer
    - Rigger
    - Stylist
    - Physio/Masseuse
    - Truck driver

The Crew

So far we have met the artist manager, the booking agent, the promoter (and his or her representatives). All these people are directly involved in putting on a modern music performance. You may never meet them directly (apart from perhaps the promoters rep) but you will meet two types of crew people: *house/local crew* and *touring/visiting* crew. House/local crew are the people employed to work directly for the venue; usually venues with in-built sound and lights, so usually at bar- to theatre- level venues. Touring crew, as you see later on in this chapter, work either directly for the band or for a tour equipment supplier (audio, lights, video etc). These are the people who will interest you – this is the kind of work you want!(figure 2.08).

House/Local Crew

The main person working on a show from the house/venue crew will be the audio technician. This person is employed to set up, run, and maintain the venue's sound system for visiting acts. If you are playing in a tiny pub or bar, if you carry your own PA, or if you create un-amplified music, then you will probably not meet the venue's audio technician (a.k.a. the "house sound guy"). If, on the other hand, you create music that needs to be amplified—in other words, pretty much any contemporary music—then the house engineer will help you when you arrive to perform your show. Do not assume I am only talking about small-capacity (150 to 700 people) venues with in-house sound equipment here. If you perform or work on a stage at an outdoor festival, then you will be working with the house guys. Their house is a tent, but they are still there to supply sound services to the incoming acts, regardless of whether you are the audio engineer.

The house audio tech is there to place microphones and monitor wedges that will amplify the bands instruments and enable the musicians to hear themselves on stage. He or she then will mix the band's sound. Bear in mind the house guy also has to do the same for all the other bands on the bill that night, which hopefully will only total two acts. (Unfortunately this will probably mean four or five bands on "local band" or talent nights.)

The other people you will find yourself working with in the venue are the local stagehands or 'humpers'. These people are employed by the venue and/or the promoter specifically to assist the touring or visiting crew with load in and load out of the PA, lights (if applicable), and the musicians equipment - speaker cabinets, amplifiers, drums, keyboards and stands; known as the 'backline'. (On larger shows the local crew will be employed to load in all the set, staging, lights, PA, wardrobe, catering, and production equipment. A typical large theatre/arena-type show will involve about 20 to 40 local crew for each load in and load out.)

If you are working as an opening act on a large show, you might not see the stagehands because their work will have been done by the time you arrive for sound check. It is common practice, however, to retain two to four local crew members to help load in the opening band's equipment and then to assist with changing over the support band's equipment during the show. This will probably be your first contact with the local crew if you are working for an opening act. The local crew will appear side-stage as the band you work for finish their performance, and then they will help take your equipment offstage in preparation for the next band coming on stage.

Many venues in the US are regulated through IATSE (International Alliance of Theatrical Stage Employees, Moving Picture Technicians, Artists and Allied Crafts of the United States), and you are therefore not allowed to load/unload your own equipment. The unloading, loading, and carrying of all the visiting production equipment has to be done by a workforce designated by the local union.

Note: Do not carry your own gear. When you arrive at a larger show, you should not automatically load in your equipment. A good tip is to send someone inside and inquire as to whether there are any local crew people to assist you. Why carry your gear on your own when someone is being paid to help you?

After your band has performed, the local crew will help you get your gear offstage to make way for the next band. They will also help you load out the gear and pack your van/car/bus. Remember, they have nothing to do with the other acts and are paid as part of running the show. These guys were probably there at 8:00 in the morning and will work at the venue until 2:00 the next morning; they still have to have to tear down PA and lights and pack big smelly trucks. My advice for dealing with local crews is to be bloody nice to them! Always make sure you ply local crews with band T-shirts, water, and whatever else they might like. (There will more information about stagehands/local crew in Chapter 4.)

Runners

Other vital members of the local crew are the runners. The equivalents of "gofers" (as in "go for this, go for that") from the film world, runners are local people with access to transportation who can therefore go on errands for the band's production personnel.

The runner will make himself or herself known to the arriving production during load in. The runner will put up a blank shopping list in the production office or dressing room, along with their cell number. If you need something during the day, such as musical equipment spares, photocopying, batteries, or laundry, you either phone the runner or write your request on the list, along with your name. The runner will then go and purchase whatever is necessary, having been given a cash float by the tour/production manager or tour accountant.

Security

Any gathering of people has to be prepared in case of an emergency. This includes modern concerts, whether classical orchestral or alternative rock. The role of the security and stewarding personnel is primarily to oversee and assist with the safety of the audience if and when and emergency should occur. When attending any modern concert, you will see these security people at the public entrances and exits and also in the "pit" (the area in front of the stage between the stage and the crush barrier). The promoter and/or venue pay for these security personnel. Most countries that stage entertainment events have very strict laws regarding the amount and type of security personnel and stewards that have to be supplied for each event. Although the majority of security people at a large show or festival are employed on a casual basis, the companies that supply security and stewarding teams provide full-time and highly trained experts to oversee the casual labour at each event.

Security personnel are also used to guard other areas of the venue, such as the dressing rooms and areas containing expensive sound, light, and video equipment, as well truck and bus parking areas. Access to these areas is based on a pass system, with the passes being issued by the tour/production manager, in conjunction with the promoter. The touring band and crew will usually have laminated passes ("laminates") that will specify the wearer has "Access to All Areas" or 'AAA'. AAA personnel may have "escort" privileges, meaning they can escort non-AAA guests or workers into areas that are off limits to non-AAA personnel.

Opening acts, guests, photographers, promoter's reps, and other working personnel are given sticky passes that indicate their role on the day and the access privileges they hold. (figure 2.09).

Figure 2.09. Sticky passes given to non-touring personnel on the day of the show.

To avoid confusion, the security personnel on the day will be given a pass sheet. A pass sheet is a copy of the passes issued on the day, arranged on one or two sheets of paper with detailed explanations of the access levels for each pass. This pass sheet is then issued to all relevant security personnel and also posted at every "sensitive" access point. This way, the security personnel can check each and every pass against the pass sheet, and allow the holder to enter areas as designated by their pass.

Audiences, crew, and band members alike all have opinions and stories about security people, most of them negative. Although the scope of this book does not allow me to really address views and complaints from the concert-going public regarding security/stewarding personnel, it is a perfect place to lay down a few truths for all the bands and crews out there that have a less-than-favourable view toward security and stewarding at shows.

Truth 1: Venue security people are employed to protect you.

Truth 2: Venue security people are employed to make sure your expensive sound/light/video/recording/catering/production equipment does not get stolen or damaged.

Truth 3: Truth's 1 and 2 are true.

What I am saying is that there really is no attempt to create any kind of inner sanctum or exclusive world when issuing passes and employing venue security staff. Pass-based controls are put in place to limit the number of people who have access to certain areas at a show or event for both health and safety reasons. Having a pass to a backstage area of the show does not mean you are any more important than anybody else viewing or participating in the running of the show. Having this kind of accreditation merely means you are necessary or accountable to the band's organization or you are amicable or trustworthy.

It may be necessary for acts to travel with their own security/close protection personnel. You have read stories or seen videos of divas and hip-hop luminaries being escorted by these "man mountains." Those are just the stories that make it into the press; nearly all acts that are capable of selling out venues of 5000 or above will employ some kind of close-protection or security logistics personnel. It is an unfortunate sign of the times that celebrities from all entertainment fields may be threatened; the music world is no different. "It happens a lot," says Steve Head from Headline Security Management. "[We] get the police involved if we know there's a stalker around" [5].

In my experience, close protection security employed by bands act more as travel/movement coordinators; this helps to take the pressure off the tour manager. Touring security are also good at explaining the rules of the road to opening bands and local crew and can read the riot act to misbehaving band members if necessary.

Touring/Visiting Crew

We have looked at the house/local crew. There is also a massive list of people who accompany a band on tour. It is important to stress that no-one is more important than anyone else on a tour. The roles vary and here are a few job descriptions of the main roles you may aspire to. (The Appendix 1 gives even more information about various touring roles.)

Tour Manager

The tour manager does the advance planning of the tour and then travels with the band for the duration of the tour. The tour manager's job on-the-road varies enormously depending on the type and success level of the act for which she is working.

Here are some of the day-to-day responsibilities of a tour manager:

- Overseeing on-time hotel departures of band and crew.

- Settling accommodation bills of band and crew.

- Overseeing travel arrangements i.e. band and crew onto the bus or to the airport in good time.

- Paying per diems to band & crew.

- Overseeing venue arrival - double checking hospitality and technical arrangements.

- Arranging up to date running order with venue and promoter.

- Overseeing promotional activities i.e. TV, radio and press interviews at the venue or at other locations.

- Supervising any support or opening acts.

- Ensuring venue is ready to open on time by supervising sound check times.

- Liaising with transport department regarding the next days' travel.

- Ensuring all acts perform on time and for the allotted time.

- Settling performance fee with promoter and collecting any

due cash.

- Ensuring all touring equipment is re-packed and loaded back onto tour transport.

- Preparing band and crew schedule sheets for the next day.

- Overseeing band and crew on to appropriate over night transport or to next hotel.

- Reporting this show's attendance figures to management and booking agent.

The tour manager of the headline act is the primary contact for any opening band and its crew. If you are working for an opening band either as a one-off or as part of a tour, you should take the time to introduce yourself to the TM of the headline act (preferably before the first day of the tour) and supply him or her with all relevant information. This should consist of:

- The number of people in your touring/show entourage. (Do not forget your drivers)

- The role of each person in your touring entourage.

- A contact number for you/your tour manager.

- The type of vehicle(s) for you and your gear.

An input list, stage plan, and any special production equipment you may be bringing for the show, such as backdrops, banners, lasers, and so on.

On arrival at the first show, make time to briefly introduce yourself and then get the hell out of the way. If you are part of a tour, there will be plenty of time for socialising later.

Audio Crew

You may be working in a venue with in-house sound and lights (100 to 1,000 capacities). You may be working on a show where the promoter or headline act has bought in its own (rented) PA system. (Venues greater than 2,000 capacity rarely have an in-house sound system.) Either way, the band may have its own crew, or there will certainly be the house crew or the system crew. (The PA supplier will send along technicians when supplying a PA system for the tour or event. Because they work for the supplier, they are the "system crew.")

You probably won't have much to do with the other artist's audio crew but, as mentioned, you will work with the house/system crew. Local crew will help you get your gear on stage, and the house/ system crew will place microphones and monitor wedges. Hopefully you will have provided them with an input list well in advance. (An input list is a list of all the instruments you use, what microphones or DI boxes you need, plus other specific audio information.) The house/system crew will also mix your monitor/stage sound and the FOH sound for bands that do not travel with their own engineer.

Backline Crew

These are the boys and girls who tend to the personal instruments, amplifiers, and effects of the band musicians themselves (figure 2.10). When working for an opening act you will often find that by the time you arrive the headliners backline crew will often have filled the stage with the band's gear, plus toolboxes, "guitar worlds," (areas at the side of the stage that the backline crew use to set up, tune and maintain guitars and basses), and production cases. You will have to negotiate what space you can have to set up your gear with them.

Figure 2.10. A backline technician striking a pedal board after sound check.

Again, if you have spoken to the TM and/or backline crews of all the bands on the bill in advance, you may be able to negotiate sharing equipment and stage space.

Always be prepared to change your setup to fit in with their existing production. For example, if the headline act's keyboard rig is stage left, then all the DI boxes for their keyboards, monitor wedges, and so on will be there at stage left. Providing outputs, power, and monitors for you is going to be time consuming if your keyboard stage setup is stage right. And time is one thing you are really short of if you want to get all your gear on stage and obtain a decent sound check. To save this time and technical hassle for the house/system crew, you should consider changing your setup to stage left. Then you can simply set up your rig in front of the existing keyboard setup; the house/system crew will only have to extend a few cables and move a monitor speaker. Voila! Everyone is happy, and you are set up and able to sound check in minutes. Make sense, doesn't it?

Lighting Crew

The lighting crew is split into two types in the same way as the audio crew—there are people who work directly for the band, and then there are house/system crew who work in the venue or tour with the rented lighting rig. A large tour (700-person capacities and upward) will often carry its own lighting equipment. This will supplement or replace the existing house lighting system. The headline act will be renting this system, and the promoter will be contributing to this cost as per his contracted agreement to "supply PA and lights to the artist's specifications." The headline act and crew has arranged, designed, trucked, and set up this system. Because the show will contain special effects and set pieces, the opening acts will probably not be given access to the full range of lights in the system. Common practice for support bands is for the lighting operator to light those acts using the generic PAR-type lights, which will be controlled by one of the touring system crew. On a large tour with a touring rig, opening acts will probably be asked to pay for one of the system crew to operate the lights for them during their show. However, I would always argue against this charge and simply and politely ask for a static "wash" for the whole of your set (figure 2.11). This is because the system crew will not know the material, will only have some general lamps to work with and so any opening band are not going to get much of a lighting show. (A 'wash' is a mix of colours from the lights that will simply illuminate the stage i.e. the lights will wash over you.)

Figure 2.11. A ground-supported lighting rig containing generic fixtures used to give a lighting 'wash'.

Video Crew

The use of video content on screens has become a staple of touring productions. The technology involved in creating and reproducing video content has evolved from delicate, heavy, complicated and expensive equipment into inexpensive packages designed for touring. The distinction between lighting and video is also blurring - video screens can be used as lighting sources and modern fixtures such a PixelLine LED strips can have video content shown through them (figure 2.12).

Figure 2.12. PixelLine LED strips in action.

Caterers

Okay, you can lose your patience with the headliner's backline people or insult the tour manager. There is one set of people, however, whom you should approach on your knees and hail as gods—the caterers!

On a large-scale show (700-capacity and upward), it is common practice to bring in people to cook hot, highly nutritious meals for the bands, the touring crew, and (occasionally) the local crew. This catering crew either tours with the act or is locally sourced for each venue. In both cases, the catering crew starts work extremely early and finishes late. Caterers have to bring in ovens, gas bottles, fridges, flatware, ice machines—everything. They cook three main meals a day, as well as provide running buffets for up to 250 people a day, depending on the size of the production. And the food is always amazing, considering the environment it is prepared in. Many of the world's venues are not very good for producing music shows, let alone cooking in.

I mention all this because, as with all modern show production, there is etiquette. Actually, it is just plain manners.

Three things to remember when filing into 'catering' (the area in the venue where the food is served):

- These people are not your Mom, and it is not a commercial restaurant. These people got up at 7:00 a.m. and will not finish until 1:00 a.m. It really is tough if you do not like what they have prepared. If you have a major dietary concern, then you have to inform someone well in advance—such as your tour manager.

- Catering is the heart and soul of any touring show or one-off event. People come here to meet up, to eat, to talk, and to relax. Be really careful what you say here, especially if you are thinking of bitching about someone. Save that for your own transportation, your hotel room, or for when you have finished the tour.

- Clear your plates, cutlery, and waste when you have finished. Again, the caterers are not your Mom, and it is not a commercial restaurant.

You may think I am overdoing it with the advice here. Unfortunately I have worked with people who had no respect or manners for anyone on the show. As I keep saying, you only get one shot at making an impression. If someone is going to put that much hard work into something as integral to life, health, and happiness as your food, then you had better show them some respect.

How do you join these people on-the-road?

You should now have a complete picture of who does what on-the-road and, more importantly, how the concert industry works. (This understanding is important – knowing your industry will stand you in a better position when you actually come to finding work).

However, you still do not know how these people got started or how you can get a job touring with international acts. There are hundreds of live production jobs out there, as we will see later on in this chapter. You have probably done some searching around for these jobs and have come up with very little relevant information, let alone road crew help wanted adverts.

Why live music industry jobs are never advertised

"Passionate, music loving person with desire to travel the world with rock bands needed for forthcoming world tour. Ability to tune guitars and set up amp stacks desirable, must dress in black. Top rates of pay."

If you have spent any time searching the help wanted ads, in newspapers or online, you will know that ads like the one above simply do not exist. Yet, in any major city on any given night there are numerous acts playing – acts employing all the sound, lighting, backline and management crew we have seen earlier in this chapter. Those bands performing each night may have a full tour crew or just someone helping doing the driving and carrying the road cases. In either case someone is getting paid to work for a band. Have a look yourself – go to www.pollstar.com and search in your city for tonight's date. There will be a list of at least 5 shows in your town this evening; five bands who will be employing road crew.

This basic research should show you that there is a substantial amount of road-crew work out there. It should also make you question yourself, thinking "How do I get those jobs? Why are there no adverts for all these road jobs?" I will answer the first question later in this book. As to the second, read on.

Adverts for road crew positions never appear in print (and very rarely online) for three reasons.

Firstly, the artists and their management companies do not wish to be bombarded with resumes and enquiries from the general public. The music industry is a small network serving a vast number of artists; this industry simply does not have the time and resources to sift through the hundreds of (probably irrelevant) applications a job ad would generate.

Secondly, the skills, experience and personality required for a road position are specific to the hiring band or tour. The total number of people qualified for any given position on a tour is probably 20 – 30, worldwide. It is not cost effective to advertise a job to such a tiny amount of suitable applicants.

The third, and main, reason is that the positions the bands need filled are not really jobs as you understand them.

Live music business jobs are different

In order that you understand why live music business jobs are different you have to understand that the economics of a touring band do not allow for the hiring of full-time staff. Despite what I wrote in chapter 1, the majority of bands do not make enough money from touring to retain permanent employees. If you find this hard to believe then look the costs involved for a small band playing a local show.

That local band will have to pay for rehearsals for the show, buy fresh strings, sticks and batteries, put fuel in the cars or van, photocopy set lists, pay for parking – the list of expenses is endless.

And, those costs are for just 4 guys playing a bar in their hometown, probably for a fee of $50.00. Now multiply those various costs by 100 or 1000 for a large tour or event, throw in extra costs for trucks, tour buses, sound and lighting rental and you see how little revenue per show a touring actually act makes. This is why touring acts really cannot afford to have full-time road-crew. Touring crew have specialised skills that can only be used when the band is touring. So, bands only hire crew when they are touring.

The 'jobs' in the live music production business are therefore short-term, non-permanent positions offered on a contract basis. These contracts are not advertised, as it is just not cost-effective. (See the section on 'Why live music business jobs are never advertised'). So, you may be touring with a band for two solid years but once that band goes off the road (to record a new album or for a break) the band will rarely be in a position to keep paying you. Some artists are able to pay their tour crew a 'retainer', - a monthly wage paid on the understanding that the crew will not work for another artist in the meantime, but I would doubt the business acumen of any artist manager who said they would be able to put me, as a tour manager, on a retainer. Why would you pay someone to sit around waiting for you to find him or her something to do? And, if you think about it, many smaller bands tour for maybe only 6-8 months each year. So, working full-time for just one band is a quick way to go broke. The only way to work effectively in the live music business is to be a freelancer.

The Oxford English Dictionary describes freelance as "earning money by selling your work or services to several different organisations rather than being employed by one organisation." Freelancers are self-employed. That means you are your own boss. Ninety-nine percent of the tour crew I know work as self-employed freelancers. Being freelance means we road crew are free to choose when we work and for whom. However, as we are self-employed, we have to search continuously for employment.

The live music production industry is made up of freelancers who bring specialised skills to the industry. These skills have been gained by specific training in a certain area i.e. sound or lighting or (more likely) learnt through years of actually working on the road. (Most of the people I work with in the touring industry 'fell into' working on tours. A combination of desire and an aptitude for the work meant my colleagues and I quickly established ourselves and gained more work, eventually leading to a career.) And, as yet, there is no organised career progression for live show production and no one-stop, internationally accredited training organisation.

Yet today's multi- billion industry requires that you know more, be better trained and be more professional in your approach. This approach therefore goes beyond replying to help-wanted ads and sending out résumés in order to get a 'job'. Your route into road-crew work needs to be appropriate to the nature of the industry.

You need to set up your own live music freelancing business.

3 Set up your own freelance crew business

You have probably just read the title of this chapter and started to panic. After all you only wanted to learn how to gain and keep a job as touring crew. Why am I telling you to start a business? (Figure 3.01.) Surely the whole idea of working for bands on-the-road is get away from 'suits', 'nine-to-five' and 'business'?

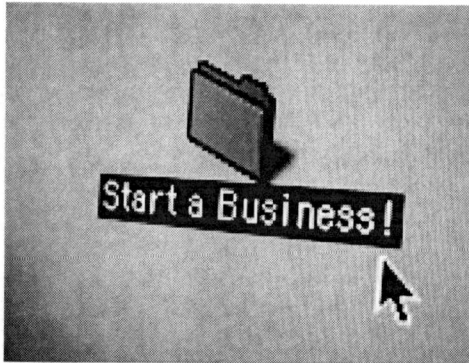

Figure 3.01. Now is the time to start your own freelance tour crew business.

Why you need to treat your career as a business

Relax, don't worry. I'm not expecting you to rent an office, hire a receptionist and start a multi-national corporation. Simply, you have to become self-employed in order to work in the live production industry. There are no full-time jobs working for bands on the road. Bands tour for a set duration, employing crew as they need them, and then come off the road to take a break, hopefully making a new album. While they are off the road the band cannot employ tour crew. Being a self-employed freelancer means you could finish one tour and then go on to work for many different bands, tour after tour, one after another; going where the work is.

Being self-employed therefore means you do not have an employer to look after the legalities of your employment – you are responsible for generating your own income, keeping your own books/accounts, issuing contracts of employment, taking out insurance and paying your own healthcare bills and taxes. These are not responsibilities to be undertaken lightly. Failure to organise your finances, taxation and insurance obligations properly can lead to business failure, bankruptcy and even a prison sentence.

Treating your freelance career as a business will enable you to be organised, legal and successful.

Planning your freelance business

There are numerous helpful books and websites dedicated to starting your own business. A quick search on Amazon will return results about specific books on self-employment and freelancing in the creative industries. In the USA you should also go to the Small Business Administration (www.sba.gov); in the UK the Business Link network has similarly useful information (www.businesslink.gov.uk).

A common thread you will find running through these books and websites is the need to write a business plan. Research into starting a business will show you that there is an accepted form for business plans which includes, amongst other things, key management, organisational and financial data.[1] While I agree with the need for a plan, I would say to you that you do not need to produce a 10,000 word document complete with marketing plans and 5 year profit forecasts. You are starting a freelance tour crew business, not launching a multi-national conglomerate - keep your business plan relevant and realistic for the live music business.

A business plan is a plan for your freelance tour crew business and it is like a road map. Your plan should be your route to success and a reminder of where you are going if things start to go wrong. Your business plan should be accurate and simple.

You can sketch out your 'road map' on single piece of paper (figure3.02). Think about what where you are now, where you want to be and how you are going to get there. Refer to your plan when things are going well as well as when things go wrong. Update, revise and amend as you go along.

Sections of your business plan

The following sections detail the information you should initially research and include in the plan for your freelance business.

What business 'type' am I?

You should choose a legal trading structure for your new freelance business. This structure is recognised by the relevant taxation

---

[1]   See www.bplans.com for example business plans

authority and is dependant on the size and scope of your plans for the business.

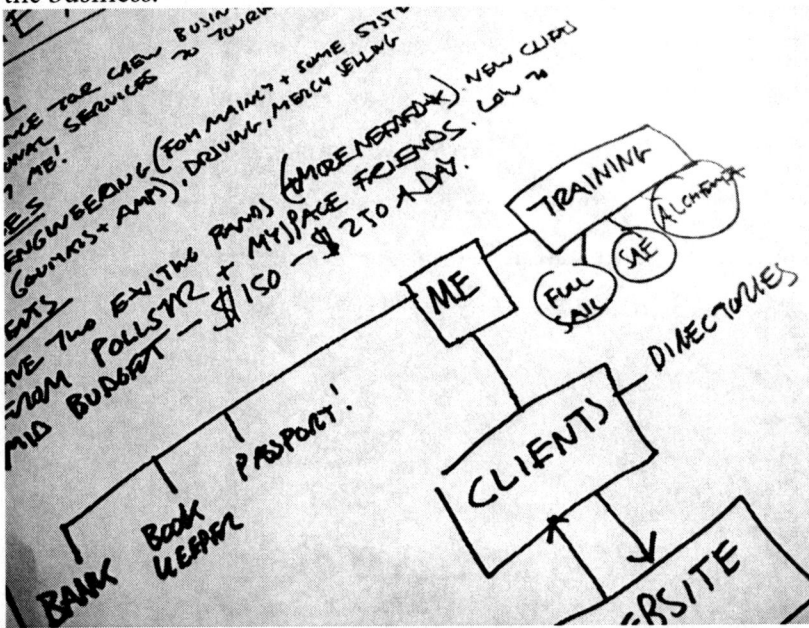

Figure 3.02. Your business plan can be a simple one-page document. Keep it handy to remind you where you are headed.

Sole trader/sole proprietor

This is one person running their own business and is definitely the simplest way to start. You keep all the profits but are also personally liable for any business debts. This means, that in the event you can't pay bills associated with your business, your creditors (people you owe money to) can seize your personal possessions (car, stereo, even your house) in order to get some money from you.

Partnerships

Like two or more sole traders running a company together. Profit is divided between the partners; each partner is also equally liable for any business debt (see 'Sole trader/sole proprietor' above).

Limited Liability Partnerships (LLP)

A partnership structure that protects the partners from any liability for the business's debt. LLC's are complex and have costly set-up fees. However your personal assets (car, stereo, house) cannot be seized to pay for company debts.

Limited Companies/PLC's/Corporations

Very simply these companies are owned by the shareholders – the 'boss' works for those shareholders, does not directly receive the profits and cannot sell the company. However, management and employees are not liable for the company's debts. Limited companies/PLC's and corporations are expensive to set up and have onerous legal and taxation responsibilities.

Which business 'type' to choose

I would advise starting your freelance business as either a sole trader/proprietor or partnership. All you need is to choose a trading name, inform your taxation authority that you are now a sole trader (very important) and you are in business! As your business grows you can change the type.

Help and advisors

The next stage in your planning is to research and identify who you are going to use for help and advice. A more formal business plan would include details of your lawyers, accountants, insurers and consultants. These are not necessary for planning a freelance crew business.

The only person you really need at the start of your business is a good book-keeper. Starting a new live production freelance business can be a hectic time, one in which it is easy to overlook the small, but important, details such as keeping your receipts and paying invoices. Neglecting these will cause you many, many problems further down the line. You may be making lots of money but is your business in good financial health?

This is where a book keeper comes in – to keep your business healthy. Bear in mind that a book keeper is not the same thing as an accountant. Many small business owners do employ an accountant to take care of their year end tax returns, and quite rightly so. However, what usually happens is that they just turn over a shoe-box full of receipts to their accountant at the year-end. The accountant will then charge them a huge amount of money to sort through the disorganised pile of bills and receipts. Aside from the massive cost, this system (or lack of) also gives the small business owner no idea of the day-to-day financial health (or otherwise) of their business (see 'Cash Flow' below). That is why you should hire a book-keeper. They are less expensive than an accountant, and can help you keep in touch with your finances. She can come in for a few hours a week (or after each period of touring) to check over your receipts, enter the figures into a record keeping system and, most importantly, chase outstanding invoices for you.

You can find a good book-keeper by looking in your local

business listings or, better still, asking other small businesses and freelancers who they use. You should only need to see your book-keeper for a couple of hours a week at the most.

It is true that having a well-ordered book-keeping system will not get you loads of road crew work; not having one will probably lead you to financial ruin.

Other advisors and sources of help you may consider are an accountant, a sympathetic bank manager, a financial advisor, and local government organisations. They will be able to advise you on all aspects of your road crew business, dependent on the thought you have put into your business planning.

Financing your business

The financial aspects of your business will be the most important part of your plan. You need to work out what you need to start your freelance business, how much it is going to cost on a day-to-day basis, and where you are going to get the money to pay for it all.

Start up costs

The good news is that starting your own live music industry business should not cost a great deal. Certainly you do not need to manufacture products, hold stock or buy raw materials. There are no employees to hire (yet) and most services you need (such as your book-keeper) can be hired by the hour.

However, you write down all your possible start up expenses and study them to see how you can afford them, however inexpensive they may appear (figure 3.03).

Most people moving from employment to starting a self-employed business will be able to draw on various 'pots' of money to tide them over until the first paychecks roll in. These pots could include any savings you have, funding from grants or loans and promises of cash from future work you are going to do. The most important source of early-stage cash for your business is likely to be an overdraft from your bank. I would advise you get an over-draft facility straight away. Work out a worst-case scenario for your finances using your business plan and then approach your bank (See 'Cash Flow' below). Remember that as a sole trader/proprietor you are personally liable for any debt – even if it is business related.

CATEGORY	ITEM	AMOUNT	NOTE
Premises	Apartment rent	$600	Working from home for 3 months
Utilities			
	Gas	$150	for 3 months
	Electricity	$150	for 3 months
	Telephone	$90	for 3 months
	ISP	$90	for 3 months
	Cell	$300	for 3 months
Financial and legal			
	Book keeper	$150	for 3 months
	Public Liability Insurance	$400	
Marketing			
	Web site	-	MySpace
	Brochures	$160	
	Directory listing	$150	for 3 months
	Business card	$75	
Equipment		$250	Headphones, Mag-Lite, multi tool etc
Misc		$200	Office stuff
	TOTAL	$2,765	

Figure 3.03. Typical start-up costs for a freelance tour crew business. Note I have factored on paying bills for three months before any income is received.

You will find it very difficult to operate effectively in the early stages of your new live music business without an overdraft but be careful set a sensible overdraft limit.

Note: Public Liability Insurance. One cost you should definitely include is that for insurance, especially 'Public Liability' insurance. You are liable for medical and legal costs if a member of the public, your client or someone else who works for your client is hurt or killed as a result of something you do while working. Likewise you are liable if you damage or lose a piece of the client's equipment or property. Public liability insurance protects you from having to pay these costs if there is an accident. More and more live production suppliers (sound, light and staging companies) now require the freelancers they hire to have this kind of insurance. Public liability insurance can be very expensive, especially for people involved in entertainment industries. You should check with your union as they may be able to negotiate a good deal from an insurer.

Cash flow

Business people always say, 'cash is king'. You know what? They are right! A business with plenty of cash can survive even if it is not making a great deal of profit. Conversely a business with no cash reserves will not survive - even if it is making a profit. Your freelance tour crew business will be no different. As an example, figure 3.04a shows the 'profit' on paper for a business selling $1000 of goods or services a month. Looks healthy doesn't it? But the figures do not take into account when money actually comes in to your account and so may be slightly deceptive.

ITEM	Month 1	Month 2	Month 3	Month 4	Month 5	Month 6
Sales	$1,000	$1,000	$1,000	$1,000	$1,000	$1,000
Costs	$500	$500	$500	$500	$500	$500
Sub-total	$500	$500	$500	$500	$500	$500
plus b/f from last month	$0	$500	$1,000	$1,500	$2,000	$2,500
Profit	**$500**	**$1,000**	**$1,500**	**$2,000**	**$2,500**	**$3,000**

Figure 3.04a. A profit statement – looks fairly healthy doesn't it?

Cash flow' is the way of measuring when you are going to receive money from the people who owe it to you and when you need to pay other people for goods and services. It is the lifeblood of your business; plenty of cash coming in regularly means you don't have to worry about paying your bills. Having to wait 30, 60 or even 90 days for your customers to pay you means either a) have to wait 30, 60 or 90 days to pay your bills or b) borrow money to pay your bills. Borrow too much money and you are in danger of still being in debt when you eventually do get paid by your customers (figure 3.04b).

Pay attention to your cash flow and plan for it before you start your new freelance business. The manner in which invoices are paid is particularly different in the live music industry (as we saw in the section about tour support in Chapter 2). My advice would be to assume your invoice will not be paid for at least 90 days and then have enough cash to survive that long.

ITEM	Month 1	Month 2	Month 3	Month 4	Month 5	Month 6
Sales	$0	$0	$0	$1,000	$1,000	$1,000
Costs	$500	$500	$500	$500	$500	$500
Sub-total	-$500	-$500	-$500	$500	$500	$500
plus b/f from last month	$0	-$500	-$1,000	-$1,500	-$1,000	-$500
CASH	-$500	-$1,000	-$1,500	-$1,000	-$500	$0

Figure 3.04b. The same business, measured according to when money is actually paid into the bank. Costs are the same but the business would be bust in six months.

A good tactic to keep your cash flow er, flowing, is to charge a percentage of your invoice up front or (in the case of a long tour) charge monthly. The business managers of a band I recently toured with set me up on the band's payroll. This meant I got paid weekly during the tour. Check to see if your client can do the same.

Timing

Planning your new live production crew business is going to take time. Don't rush. You should include a time scale of action into your plan.

You are probably impatient to get going but I would recommend you spend at least the next six months researching and planning your new career as a freelancer. During that time you can start to undertake small contracts for new clients – you should be able to fit these in around your existing day job commitments - especially as most shows take place in the evening. In any case you should definitely have 2 or 3 clients, contracts or tours lined up for when you finally take the plunge and go full-time self-employed. Figure 3.05 shows a sensible time line.

Your plan should never be really finished – as I said it is a road map to help you get where you want to go. However at some point you should be confident that your business can work and that you now have your own live music industry business. Part of this confidence will come from knowing there are customers out there – customers who are willing to hire you for their tours or events. In order to get hired you need to provide the skills and expertise those customers need.

Roadie, Inc 6 months plan

6 Months to go.

Research clients. Buy music industry directories. Build Wordpress site and Facebook, Twitter and LinkedIn pages. Hit up network. Register business with tax authority. Make sure on top of existing work commitments. Research any funding . Take on a couple of freelance jobs.

5 Months to go.

Take on more freelance jobs. Find a book keeper and/or accountant. Open business bank account.

4 Months to go.

Continue to build up customers. Do some local advertising and keep the network informed about work. Make sure invoices go out.

3 Months to go.

Get book keeper to chase up outstanding invoices. Check progress of business bank account.

2 Months to go.

Scale back existing job commitments (go part time?). Hit up existing clients for referrals and testimonials. Leaflets and brochure? SAVE ALL CASH!

1 Month to go.

Quit day job! Make sure new clients pay up-front for next two months.

Figure 3.05. Allow about 6 months to fully launch your new business.

4   Getting started

Having started your road map to a freelance tour crew business you may be asking yourself "how do I actually get started on-the-road?" You are not alone; I get at least a couple of emails a week from prospective freelance tour crew. Most of the questions I answer involve information about career paths and training courses i.e. 'what do I need to know to get a job on-the-road' or where 'can I train to be a tour manager/ roadie/ crew person?"

Unfortunately there is no recognised career path or association to guide freelance live production crew. My colleagues and I have followed a varied path to get where we are today - the common theme amongst all of us is that there isn't a common theme! There is no easy way to start a career in this industry. So, with no simple route to follow, how do start off as a freelance crew person?

Get to know local talent.

When it comes to getting started as an on-the-road crew person I have one, all-time number one tip: get to know local talent. When I am asked 'how do I become a tour manager/ roadie/ crew person', I simply always say – find yourself a band! The biggest and most successful of bands/artists need the best crew; crew who have skills, expertise and years of experience. But you may not have that experience right now. And, to be fair to you, you are not going to get a touring job with a national touring band if you have no experience, no reputation and no recommendations.

That should not stop you though. You need to enter the industry, now. So Find yourself a band and grow with them (figure 4.01).

Let me give you an example. Anthony Oates is a backline technician whose clients include Nick Cave and the Bad Seeds, Goldfrapp, Tindersticks, Roni Size Reprezent and Apollo 440. "I used to work in a club so I knew lots of the local bands, including one who had just got a (record) deal." says Anthony. "They started doing lots of gigs and I used to tag along in the van, sitting on the gear in the back (no tour buses in those days). After a while they got fed up of me drinking all their beer so they decided to give me some something to do, carrying their gear and tuning their guitars." [9]

Anthony started with one, unsigned band. He has now been working full-time in the industry for over 20 years.

It really is that simple. It may not be *easy* but it is a *simple* process. Find the best, emerging talent in your town, area, or venue and make yourself indispensable to them. For example, the musicians you find, know or work with may not be technically orientated. If you have experience and training in the technical operation of a concert then you will be able to help these people.

Figure 4.01. The young bands of today are the superstars of tomorrow; make sure you are on their team.

Ask yourself:

- How many times do you hear bands you know complaining about house sound engineers or about weird 'feedback/ howl round, bad stage sound or inattentive bar managers?

- How many times are musicians late for shows and sound checks?

- How many times do band members forget or break their instruments, and assume they are able to borrow other band's equipment?

Can you see the potential here? With a little forethought and technical ability you can make yourself indispensable to all the 'little' bands in your town. (And in fact, those bands may not be so little; they may be on the verge of signing to an international record deal – you just don't know it yet).

Then take this one step further. Say a band you befriend is playing a show out-of-town or out-of-state. What would a group of musicians, tired and far from home, pay to have someone with them who had organisational or technical skills? My guess (based on considerable experience), is that they would give or pay a lot to the right person.

That person could be you.

If you are in any doubt yourself that this may be true then let me say that many years ago that person was me. That is why I recommend this route to a road crew career because, like many of my colleagues, I started out by helping fellow local musicians and the bands I knew from my home town. The work was hard and I was not that well paid but I had skills that other people needed and, more importantly, I learnt new skills. My career grew from there; I needed to prove my worth before I could progress but I made the right choices by making myself indispensable to those local music artists.

Many of my colleagues followed the same route. "I have been touring for around seven and half year's now." says 'Supa' Dave Rupsch, Production manager and FoH engineer for My Chemical Romance. "I started working in a club mixing sound for a tiny, and I mean tiny, amount of money. My touring career started when a band came through who needed a sound guy, I dropped everything and went on the road with them" [10].

Getting to know local talent involves making your self known to the people in your area who are also 'going places' -bands and musicians who are likely to make the break to national or international touring. You should cultivate contact with your people and build up your network.

Build up your network.

You have started your own freelance crew business and so now you should have a network. Yes, I know what you are saying:

"I do not have a network – I'm just starting out in this business"

Or "I live in the middle of nowhere, there is no network here"

Or "I am still at school".

So, you may feel that you have 'no network'. Whatever you feel about your situation I would strongly disagree that you have no live music business network. A network is everyone you know – it just happens that some of these people will be useful in establishing your new career. You would be surprised at the amount of people you already know who can help. Forget about power lunches and business clubs; you have people around you right now who can help you, all you have to do is ask them for advice and help. Still not convinced you have a network? Ask yourself:

- Do you go to shows?

- Do you know people in bands or DJs?

- Are you friends with other bands and Djs on Facebook and Twitter?

- Do you know people who work in clubs, bars or record store staff?

- Are you a member of clubs and associations at college?

- Is your best friend/cousin/neighbour someone in the music business?

If you can answer yes (or maybe) to any of these questions then you have a network, a network that is applicable to what you want to achieve.

Use your network

You should identify what you help you need from your network. This could include:

- Finding out which bands and DJs from your area are playing shows and letting them know you are available to help.

- Advertising your freelance services in local musical instrument shops, rehearsal studios, record stores and venues. Use. Use your network to find the right places to advertise.

- Ensuring your network of venue managers, promoters,

rehearsal rooms and music instrument stores know that you are looking to set up a freelance tour crew business.

- Use Twitter, Facebook, and LinkedIn to tell your network what you are up to.

This is stuff you can do, right now, regardless of where you live, where you work or go to school.

Once you have enlisted the help of your network you should, and this is *very* important, keep track of all the national touring acts coming into town. Why? Well, venue managers and promoters will often give opening slots to the best local acts. Getting an opening slot for a national touring act can be a big deal for an emerging local band and they will obviously want their show to go as well as possible. That opening band will need technical and organisational assistance but may be completely unaware as to how to find it. This is why you need to contact those local acts as you hear of their opening gigs and offer your services.

A strategy would be to pick one or two venues in your area and make sure you have subscribed to those venue mailing lists, Facebook pages and Twitter feeds for the upcoming concerts. Then check to see which local acts (if any) are opening up for the national band.

The reality of modern concert touring is that the opening act will not be publicly advertised until a couple of weeks before the event, leaving you little or no time to offer your services to that band. You therefore need to make sure you have those promising local bands in your network, or that your network can let you know when opening bands have been booked by a local promoter.

The benefit of working for local acts on opening shows is that you may well be able to fit in evening shows around any existing day job. 'Local openers' (as opening acts from your home town are known)are inevitably first on the bill and so will not be expected to load in or sound check until maybe six o'clock in the evening (assuming the standard seven o'clock venue opening time). Then, as they are first on, the local band's performance will be over by eight or nine o'clock which means a relatively early finish for you as well.

This is how I got started in my career as a freelance tour crew person. Unfortunately I was not following a plan, I simply became the person in my home to mix live sound for local acts – especially when those same acts then opened up for national acts at the larger venues. I gained lots of experience and a good reputation and could keep whatever other 'day job' I held.

You should do the same, but plan it out first. Get yourself known to local acts and when one of them starts to do well, make sure you are part of their team. The success of this small, local act may also be a stepping stone for your own career.

Obviously you will not get paid much (if anything) in the early days, especially working with an up-and-coming band. Do not be discouraged through. You have to think long-term. This investment of your time and expertise now will be worth more in the bank in the long run. A positive, can-do attitude when dealing with new bands, venue managers or local agents will get you noticed. And getting noticed is your main priority.

As 'Captain' John Jackson (Stage manager and drum technician for the All-American Rejects) told me, "There are a lot of techs out there who started out as a friend to the band, and will always be a friend to the band, but have gone on to do real well because they sought advice from other techs and bands and were willing to work hard and learn." [11]

So, if you are working in a venue as sound, lighting or stage crew make sure you are always, always nice, polite and attentive to the visiting artists – especially local support/opening acts.

The fledgling bands of today are the superstars of tomorrow and as you know, people value loyalty. That 'local' opening band could be on their way to a large record company deal with lots of tour support money. If they know you, like you and you have done a good job for them so far you could be in the perfect position for them to hire you as a touring crew member.

Being polite, attentive and professional towards the visiting artist – that is what you should be doing in your job. Or, to be more precise - work hard, be nice and learn.

Simple, really.

Training

I mentioned at the start of this chapter that you cannot really 'train' to be a tour manager or crew person. There is no real 'one-shot' school or college that can teach you the specifics of working on a rock tour.

However, as live music continues to grow as an entertainment phenomenon and as a viable source of employment, the importance of structured career training and guidance has been recognised. "Some people may think education will sanitise rock'n'roll," says Geoff Ellis of concert promoters DF Concerts. "But in important areas such as health and safety there is room to learn in a classroom environment." [12]

Modern concert production is evolving constantly and the roles of touring personnel are becoming increasingly specialised. Gone are the days of the generic 'roadie' – one person, a friend of the band, employed to drive a van, shift the band's gear and tune the guitars.

Flip back to figure 2.08 in chapter 2 and have a good look at the different roles involved in a concert. LED screen engineers, camera people, hydraulics engineers, FOH and monitor audio engineers, instrument technicians, audio systems engineers, riggers, production managers – the list of the modern touring jobs goes on. These specialised jobs are required by an ever-demanding industry. While it is true that there is still a demand for the 'jack-of-all-trades' when working with emerging acts, it is also true that you should have one skill, preferably acquired through training, in order to gain a competitive edge in this industry.

Chris Taplin, Tour/Production Manager for The Darkness, Super Furry Animals, Bjork, and Morcheeba says, "I have never trained specifically for this job, but I did study music at college. This exposed me to a lot of emerging technology of the time (MIDI and digital audio), which helped a lot when I came to 'tech' for bands. I also play a lot of instruments which makes understanding how the stage set up works a little easier than it would be for a non-player." He adds "Training is more important now that the job is becoming more technical." [13]

Courses and qualifications

Training and education are important to your career progression and care should be taken in choosing the right course or qualification. However, there is a still a great deal of resentment from sections of the live production industry as to the worth of any qualification. This is probably why 54% of touring crew says an education or training course has not helped them get work [14]. "All the résumés we receive from kids on music courses go straight in the bin," says Chris Hill from Wigwam Acoustics, a PA rental company [12].

At the same time, the live music business is becoming increasingly regulated ; the days of 'making it up as you go along' are quite clearly over. The demands and responsibilities involved in staging tours are increasing every year – this is not the kind of job you can just walk into. I would therefore recommend you get training and education that focuses on the practical elements of live crew work as well as the theory.

Colleges and courses do exist to teach technical stage craft for theatre environments; a quick search in Google will turn up courses and colleges in your area. (Search for show production courses, stage management courses and theatre technical training).

I have also found degree courses in event management which will teach you some of the skills necessary to become an effective band tour manager. It is important to have an understanding of the management behind the industry you work in (see chapter 2) and many music courses contain an element of management studies.

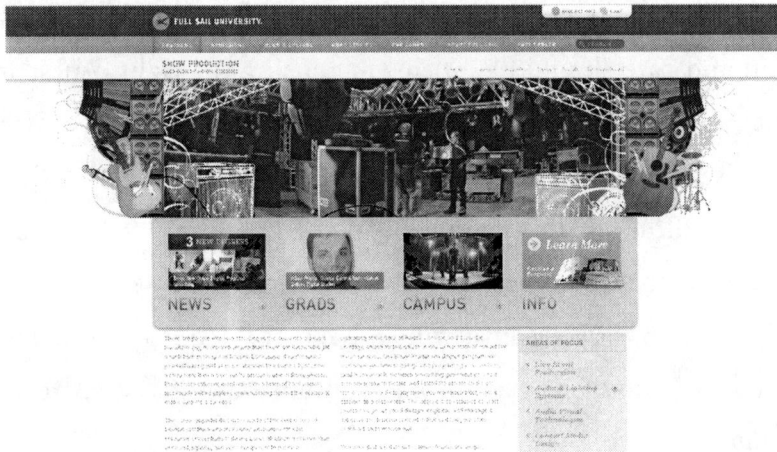

Figure 4.02. Specialised courses in live music production are common; check the course content though.

You are entering the live music business, therefore the most useful courses to look at would be something to do with live audio engineering. The audio engineering courses you research may be more studio-based i.e. the making and mixing of records. Although the audio theory may be the same (signal path etc) mixing audio for stage and recording for CD's or radio is not the same. There are also huge differences in the conventions and protocols of live audio production and so, to get the most out of any audio course, you should look for courses that specialise in audio for live music events or show production (figure 4.02).

Any course in live audio you undertake should definitely cover the following areas in some detail:

- Power – understanding voltage and amperes, different power cables and connectors and the implications of working with 3-phase power.

- Sound – how sound travels, the frequency spectrum and frequency wavelengths, Inverse Square Law as applied to audio.

- Signal path – Ohms Law, gain structure, microphone and line level amplification, inserts and auxiliaries, desk bussing and grouping, output, multi-core, stage boxes, remote boxes.

- Signal cables and connectors – XLR, NL2, NL4, NL8, EP5/6, handling and storing cables.

- Microphones – dynamic and condenser microphones, microphone pick-up patterns, phase reversal.

Note: Three things that will kill you. Working on live music events can be dangerous, training for them equally so. Remember the three things that will kill you – gravity, electricity and stupidity.

Studying and gaining any qualification shows that you have commitment and dedication. You should always mention relevant training when approaching employers or clients. The training may not be relevant to actually working in the live music industry but again, your training shows you have dedication and commitment. I take far more notice of résumés that indicate the person has attended (and passed) a college or university course.

You can still work part-time for bands or in a club while studying. In fact, most courses run by higher education colleges and universities will break for at least three months during the summer, a very busy time for live music production companies and touring bands. There is therefore opportunity for you to study, learn and earn. Even if you do not earn that much money from any work you do while studying, the experience you will gain from your actual show work will make your studies more relevant.

Always keep an open mind while training or learning – for instance, you may love lighting and be totally absorbed by the new lighting technology but please do not dismiss the audio, video and staging aspects of modern concert touring.

Try to obtain a rudimentary knowledge of other technical disciplines. You are going to be working in teams of people with a variety of skills. It is vital you know how the various components and personnel of a show fit together. For instance, as a back line technician, you should know that you would never set up all the bands backline equipment on stage before the lighting equipment has been loaded in and set up.

Books, magazines and websites

You can learn a great deal in an informal setting by reading around the subject. As well as reading this book you should make sure you subscribe or have access to industry trade magazines such as Total Production, Live! , Light & Sound International, Mix and Audience.

Web resources are springing up all the time; the touring fraternity is a keen user of social sites such as Facebook. There is also a dedicated tour crew social networking site at www.crewspace.ning. com which is well used and liked with 71% of tour crew having a listing there [14]. However, Crewspace is an invite-only network but a tour of the site can be found at http://www.crewspace.com/preview/cs-tour.php (figure 4.03).

You will find other 'backstage jobs' sites on the internet but they do not have the credibility of Crewspace. In fact my studies show

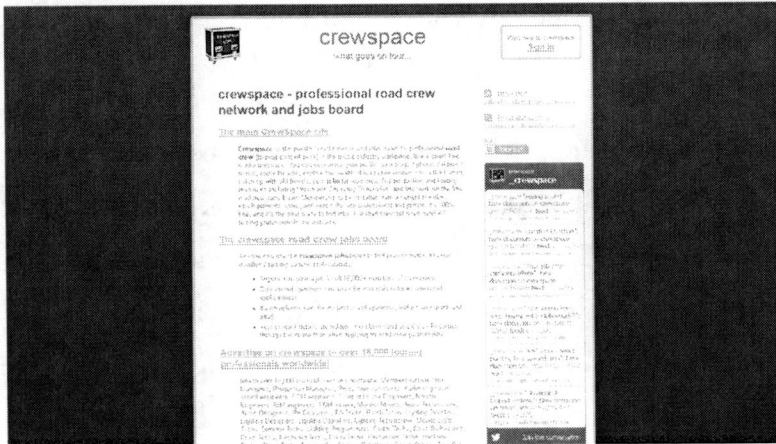

Figure 4.03. Crewspace is an online social networking site for touring road crew.

that less than 1% of touring crew have gained any paid work from sites such as roadiejobs.com or the Billboard jobs board.

Broaden your skills.

OK, you have gone out and found the 'most-likely-to-succeed' musicians and bands in your area and offered your services. You have applied for a theatre or production skills training course. That's great; you should not skip these steps. But, if you called or emailed me right now and said "What else can I do to gain and keep work in the live music industry?" I would answer:

- Are you musical? Can you play an instrument?

- Can you string a guitar, set up an amp or a drum set?

- Can you record using Pro Tools, arrange a song in Ableton Live or wire up a MIDI controller?

- Do you own or can you drive a van or truck?

If you can say yes to any of the questions above and are serious about gaining and keeping a career in the live music industry then you are in an excellent starting place already. I mentioned being trained is a fabulous way into concert touring. Specialising as a sound engineer or lighting person will eventually get you work in this industry.

My experience shows me that you will get better paid work if you also have other, relevant skills. For instance, I work primarily as a Tour Manager (TM). I can also mix FOH sound and monitor sound. I can tour as a Tour Manager, I can tour as a TM who is also doing FOH sound. Sometimes I tour as an audio engineer only. My multiple skills give me an advantage over my colleagues. Say a client calls me as she needs a tour manager for an upcoming tour. There are a couple of other people also being considered – why should she choose me? Well, I can suggest to the client that I can undertake two roles on the tour. My proposal would be that for only $x a day over my usual daily rate I can combine one or more skills, saving the client money. I will probably then win the contract for that tour.

And while you do not want to be doing two jobs for one wage, it does make sense to be able to offer other skills in order to get that contract. Many of my colleagues can double up as TM/FOH engineer or driver/back line technician.

Beyond using skills to win a contract, you should make sure you

Figure 4.04. The 'Venue' series of live mixing console (shown here) is made by Avid and is fully compatible with Pro Tools, another Avid product. (Image courtesy of Avid.)

learn basic back line skills – by this I mean stringing and tuning guitars and basses. You will be working with bands on tour, at the very least you should understand the equipment they use. Learn how drum kits are assembled (and disassembled). Talk to musicians and find out time saving hints and tips for setting up gear. Learn how to operate the most common music software (Pro Tools, Ableton, and Logic), MIDI and computer based samplers, sequencers and modules. Electronic dance music (EDM) as personified by acts such as Deadmau5, Orbital, Skrillex, and Chemical Brothers is an increasingly popular live genre, and one that is not going to go away anytime soon [21]. Make sure you keep abreast with the technology those guys are using. Also, digital control for live mixing is now commonplace so make sure you are up-to-speed with the latest technology. (figure 4.04).

Again, the trick is to make yourself indispensable to any client

– whether they be a local act struggling to get noticed or a top international touring band.

Get that experience.

The problem with any training or when starting out in a job is that you do not have the experience that makes you invaluable to your employer. It's the same old problem - you can't get the work until you have the experience and you cannot get the experience until you have worked in the industry...

How do you get around this problem?

The secret to gaining the experience is to work on shows and events doing jobs that do not require much (if any) experience. There are two crew positions that I would recommend as a starting point to further your freelance career: stagehand and merchandise seller.

Stagehand/local crew person

Stage hands/local crews are the non-touring personnel hired locally to load in and load out the masses of equipment used in modern touring productions, as described in chapter 2 (figure 4.05). The promoter or the venue will employ people directly (from their network of people they know) or use a union or agency who specialise in providing local crew.

On larger shows the stagehands will be employed to load in all the set, staging, lights, PA, wardrobe, catering and production equipment. A typical large theatre/arena type show will involve about 20-40 'local crew' each for the load in and load out.

The work of a stagehand is really, really hard involving long, unsociable hours of physical labour. You will be unpacking and packing trucks, shifting huge flight cases about and running heavy cables around venues. Physical strength is useful but stamina is the more important trait. Local crews are not paid very well(it is low-grade manual labour after all) but the job offers two important benefits for someone looking to get into freelance crew work - an insider's view of the various methods and equipment used in modern touring and direct contact with touring personnel.

Stagehands who possess any technical skills or training, work hard, are sensible and have a good attitude will soon find themselves moving away from the straight forward unpacking and packing of trucks. These stagehands will often be assigned more interesting tasks throughout the put-up process of the show because of their aptitude and attitude.

When I load into a venue I always ask the stagehand crew boss to assign the more capable and intelligent of his crew to me directly. I can then work with those stagehands, directing them to assist my sound and lighting department heads, knowing the stagehands have the relevant knowledge to really help my crew.

Stagehands are charged out to the visiting production on a time basis called a 'call'. A call is usually four hours. This means each stage hand has to be paid for four hours of their time, even if their work is finished sooner.

You might therefore work for four hours in the morning and then not work again until the call in the evening. However the more capable stagehands will often be retained after the morning call. They will then assist with setting the stage, loading in and assisting opening acts. . These stagehands are known as 'stop-ons'. Being a stop-on means very long days but more money and direct contact with the band's crew.

Figure 4.05. Stage hand - long hours and poor pay and a vital part of learning how a rock show works.

All major concert cities will have at least one crewing agency or union 'local' who will supply stagehands/'local crew' to promoters and venues. Make the necessary enquiries and sign yourself up for this kind of work. Most crew agencies insist that you are self-employed and are responsible for paying your own taxes. You may also have to join a 'local' union in order to be able to crew at certain venues in your city.

Once on the books of the organisation you should make sure you get employed on as many shows as possible. This may be difficult for you as many major cities have venues spread far and wide – you may find yourself working on shows 20 miles from where you live and travelling for an hour or more to and from work at unsociable hours. I have found however that the agency or union will try to allocate the more local people to particular venues; it makes sense to them as they want you to be able to be home early enough to get up and work on a show the next day.

Once you find yourself working regularly on local events you should buy yourself an 'AJ' (adjustable spanner) (fig. 4.06) and plenty of PVC tape. The AJ will be used to bolt the lighting truss together, which will be one of the first jobs you will do after unpacking the truck, and the PVC will be used to wrap up the cables properly at the end of the night. Having these basic tools shows you understand the job and that you are not there just to throw boxes into a back of a truck for a living.

Note – The Lighting Truss . Modern concert lighting is hung from a sub-structure, or 'grid', which is suspended from the roof of the venue/stage. This sub-structure is made up of sections of 'truss' – lightweight sections of metal frame. These sections need to be assembled before the lights can be attached and the grid hoisted into the air. This is the first job of the day for any touring production.

Finally, you should observe closely what is going on when on a call and ask lots of relevant questions.

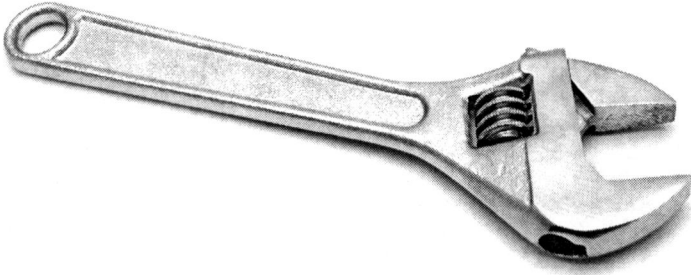

Figure 4.06. An adjustable spanner or 'AJ' – a massively useful tool for any stagehand.

Tour merchandise seller

Any band playing live should have merchandise to sell at their shows - t-shirts, hoodies, CDs and badges/pins. For many lesser known bands, selling 10 t-shirts after a show earn them more than the fee from the ticket sales and will pay for the fuel and lodgings for the night. "That's great Andy", I hear you say, "but I'm not in a band and am trying to find out how to gain and keep a career in the live music business - what has this got to do with me?"

Well I already told you that my number one tip for gaining and keeping work in the live music industry is to find those younger emerging acts and approach them with your technical and organisational skills. If you have no technical or organisational skills then they may have no use for you. However, what if you can combine your enthusiasm and positive attitude with a useful service?

One very useful service is that of selling the band's merch. Offer to sell merch for the band as well as carrying amps or driving the van. Prove yourself as reliable and trustworthy. As I said, the merchandising operation for most bands is their financial lifeblood and every band I have ever worked for has told me how important it is to them to have someone capable and trustworthy to look after their merchandising operation. And, for you, the selling of the merch means you get to work on shows, maybe even getting paid for your work. Then you will perhaps go on a tour – with little or no previous experience of touring. Don't sit back and coast along when this happens - you need to capitalise on the opportunity. Offer to help out wherever you can, and not just with the merch selling. You are only really busy as a merch seller after the audience is let into the venue so during load-in, sound check, and load-out you are free to help out - helping the band you are with, the other bands, the promoter – whoever.

The touring scene is a small, 'family' affair, so get in there and get your face well known. Once your face and reputation is known you can tout your desire to do freelance crew work to other bands.

If you cant find a band to directly sell merch for then you should approach the companies who print and supply t-shirts, posters etc that the bands sell on the road. These companies need freelance merchandisers to take care of sales on-the-road. Working for the merch company means you would not work directly for the band. You therefore may not get to meet or make friends with the actual band but merch selling still leaves you lots of time in the day when you can make yourself useful to the tour manager and crew. Use your time by volunteering to help the people in the production office.

Tour merchandisers need to be well organised and trustworthy. You also to need to have great people skills – you are the public face of the band and need to be friendly and approachable at all times. Merch selling is a great way to meet people and make friends around the world as well as advancing your touring career.

5 Getting hired

Imagine this scenario. You have set up your business, done some relevant training and got yourself known to a few local acts. One of those acts signed a record deal and went on a series of tours, taking you along with them. After a whirlwind two-year album campaign the band has stopped touring in order to write and record their next album. You have had a blast, made a lot of friends and a little bit of money. This is now your life, your career.

You want to get out on another tour as soon as possible. But how do you get onto a tour if you do not know the bands involved?

Selling your services

Before I explain how you can get onto another tour, I want to back track and explain the fundamentals of marketing or 'selling' your services to a client.

As a small business you need to convince prospective and existing clients of the need to hire you as opposed to your competitor. This persuasion should always emphasise the features of what you offer and the benefits to your client of using you. This is the selling part; putting across your superior experience, expertise, price, whatever, in order to get the work.

In his excellent book, 'Selling Your Services' [15], Bob Bly explains what he calls the 'Five-Step Service Selling Process'. This involves:

1. "Generating initial interest in your service."

2. "Follow up the initial interest to get an appointment or generate a meaningful discussion about your service."

3. "An initial meeting or discussion."

4. "Getting the assignment or project."

5. "Keeping the client 'sold' after the sale is made."

You can read further explanations of the five steps in Mr. Bly's book. One point he does make is "business buyers have to buy". Substitute 'artist manager' for business buyer and you will understand what he means. The artist's manager (or band) has to have crew for their next tour. They are 'in the market' i.e. looking for tour crew. This is not an impulse purchase; the manager will be researching the crew personnel available and making a decision. You need to make that manager interested in using you. Let's use Bly's five-step process to make that happen.

Initial interest. (a.k.a. advertising)

You are surrounded by messages and information from people trying to get you to have an initial interest in the products or services. These messages take the form of the TV, radio, print, poster and online advertisements you see every day. There are also all the marketing emails, letters, circulars and phone calls.

I am not suggesting you bombard the general public with news of your freelance tour crew business. Mass advertising of a specialised service would be inappropriate and a waste of money, as we saw in chapter 2. However, you do need to inform potential clients. To do this you should use a combination of websites social media, 'brochures' and résumés.

Web sites

Eight percent (8%) of live music business professionals – booking agents, artist managers and bands –found their tour crew last year by using the internet [14]. This might not sound like a huge amount of people until you consider that Pollstar, a live music business information service, lists more than 2400 artist management and booking companies in the US alone. This means that in 2010 approximately 200 shows or tours used crew found directly from searches using Google, Bing or Yahoo. This figure can only increase as access to the internet on mobile devices becomes easier. And this is why you must have your own web site (as well other sites such as Facebook, Myspace and Linkedin.)

A website is relatively simple to build and maintain these days. There really is no need to learn programming or graphic design in order to have an effective site. 'Effective' is the key word here – your site must give people who land on there a clear reason for wanting to hire you. Look at your page through the eyes of a prospective client – what do they need to see?

Any good website is built using 5 steps; registering a domain, finding a web host, designing the site, writing the content and optimising for the search engines.

Register a domain

The domain (and domain name) is what people will type in to their browser in order to access your site. Livemusicbusiness.com, for instance, has *livemusicbusiness* as a domain name and *.com* as the domain. The domain and name gives your site and your business its identity so choose carefully. You should also consider the impact of a top level domain such as *.com* or *.co.uk* on your business identity. Unfortunately you may find a great name is still available but not in the *.com* domain.

Registering of domain names is done via the internet itself – a quick search on Google will turn up the most popular services.

Find a web host

The web host is a company that stores your online files on their servers and makes your site available on the internet (you can host your own website if you want, but this is technically challenging as well as being very expensive). A good web host will also provide you with a set of controls to make it easier to upload your website documents and design.

There are many, many web hosting companies these days – again, a search on Google should turn up the most popular providers. Don't go for the least expensive offers though. You should check into reliability and 'uptime' scores when comparing web hosts.

Uptime is the most important as this is a measure of the total time per month that the host is available on the internet. Look for hosts with uptime scores of as close to 100% as possible. You really don't want your website disappearing for hours or days on end.

Design the site

Designing is not only deciding the layout, colours and graphics of your site but should also consider the function and intention of the site. What are you designing your website to do?

In your case, as a live music business crew person, you need to tell people who arrive at your site who you are, what you do, who you have done it for, what you can do for the visitor, how much you charge, and where they can get hold of you. This is more about words than pictures so I suggest you design a 'brochure' site – one that conveys useful information to your prospective clients. The easiest way to do this is to create a blog[1]. Don't worry; I am not expecting you to have to write reams of content or a post to your site every day. It's just that blogs and blogging software create an ideal framework to present information, are easy to set up and most are free.

Wordpress is the most popular and flexible blogging software with 25 million websites using it's free software [16]. There is an even a free hosted version at www.wordpress.com. You can set up a simple brochure site with a couple of pages of information, your résumé and contact details in a couple of minutes using a

---

1   From 'web log'.

framework such as Wordpress (www.livemusicbusiness.com uses Wordpress!)

Content

As I mentioned it's all about the words. Your prospective clients will probably use one of the major search engines (Google, Bing or Yahoo) to try to find touring crew. Search engines still look at the words on a website to determine how useful or relevant a site is to the needs of the person searching. I look at crew web sites on a constant basis and these are the things that are useful to me (and will show up in the search engine results pages):

- Description of what the crew person does – for example 'backline tech', 'FOH engineer', 'rigger'.

- A list of the clients, bands and tours the crew person has worked for.

- Any relevant training, awards or degrees.

- What they are doing right now – for example 'Available for tours until March 31st' or 'On tour in Europe until April 2012'.

- Relevant contact information – mobile/cellular number, email address.

Whatever you decide to include on your site, update it regularly (which is easy using blogging software such as Wordpress). The first contact a potential client has with you will almost certainly be through your web site – make sure that client knows exactly who you are, what you do and what you are doing at the moment.

Fig 5.01 The Complete FOH Engineer Page on Facebook

Social media

Social media refers to services such as Facebook, Twitter, MySpace, LinkedIn, Tumblr, Pintrest and (to a certain extent) YouTube. Businesses have learnt the value of social media to find and keep customers – you should do the same.

You probably have a MySpace or Facebook profile already. Your profile must reflect the professional nature of what you are offering as a freelance tour crew business. If your page is currently focused on the more personal elements of your life (your favourite amusing videos or blogs about kayaking for instance) then either remove those elements or, in the case of Facebook, start a new Page.

Facebook pages are a way for businesses and services to interact with Facebook users (955 million plus at this time of writing [17]). You can post updates, news and photos once you have set up your page just as you would with your profile. The Complete FOH Engineer is a good example of this (Figure 5.01)

Social media is good way to attract new clients but you should also make sure you get invited to join Crewspace.com. It is a terrific network providing help, support and advice for touring crew (see chapter 4).

'Brochures'

I have put the word 'brochures' in inverted commas as I am referring to any kind of sales material – flyer, rate card, brochure, pamphlet, letter or PDF – that you send to a potential client who asks for further information.

It used to be that the only way to learn more about a company was to ask for a brochure. After seeing or hearing an advert you would call that company or fill in a mail-in card and the sales materials would be sent to you. Increased access to information via the Internet has diminished the importance of such materials - yet they are still a very useful thing to thing to send. Not only do brochures provide that little extra personal service to a potential client, they act as an indicator to the amount and type of clients interested in your service. For example, say a client calls or emails you saying she heard about you via a colleague and wanted some more information. You send her your standard sales material (whatever that may be, more on this later). By doing this, you have taken two important steps towards getting more work. Firstly you have given a potential client the information she needed, which may or may not answer her questions and prompt her to hire you. Secondly, and perhaps more importantly, you now have the contact details of a new client. Even if she does not hire you this time around you have her details and can call, email or send letters to her as part of a marketing campaign in the future.

Brochures help to 'pre-qualify' your clients – the ones who are really interested in you are easier to contact (they asked you for information) and are more likely to hire you.

What type of brochure should you use and what should it contain?

The most effective brochure is a single-page two-sided letter. This can be sent in a glossy card cover complete with photos and your logo if you wish. The letter can then be posted, faxed or emailed as an attachment. (In fact you will probably send more attachments than postal responses. Your letter should be converted to PDF format – you can do this easily using the free OpenOffice software found at www.openoffice.org.)

As this is a response to a request for information your letter should contain extra information to that already listed on your web site. The benefits of your service, common problems the client may have (that you can help solve) and detailed pricing information could all be included in your brochure.

Résumés

You may be wondering, as a person running a business, why you would send out a résumé? Surely résumés are used by people looking for jobs?

Well, you may run your own freelance tour crew business but a résumé is still a very useful tool. 80% of music industry professional that I surveyed expect to see a résumé from a potential supplier [14]. It is still the accepted way of receiving information about someone and, even if you are using advertising and mail-outs, you should still have a well prepared résumé available for clients who may request one. However, because you are using your résumé to enhance information your client may have already, you need to make sure your résumé is in the correct format.

Chronological résumé

Figure 5.03 shows a chronological résumé. As you can see the résumé lists the persons career/job achievements with the most recent at the top.

Rhoda Crew

6 Arcadian Road, Boxley, Kent AD1 1AA
D.O.B 15/10/84
Home Tel: 020 3038
Mobile Tel: 07972 243
rhodcrew@yahoo.com

WORK EXPERIENCE

National Accounts Co-ordinator *Mega Music, London*
September 2007 to April 2009
Produced Sales department release and competitor schedules
Point of contact for all Sales department enquiries
Managed single and album sales notes for distribution
Approved and supplied artwork for adverts

Sales and New Media *CIA Records, London*
July 2003 to September 2007
Produced all Sales department schedules and midweek reports
Point of contact for all Sales department enquiries
Managed single and album sales notes for distribution
Sent out relevant artwork and advertising tagging to label accounts

Creative Department *Worldwide Music, London*
April 2000 to June 2007
Liaising with photographers, stylist, managers, editing suites and directors in order to
meet deadlines for photo shoots and video sessions
Re-cataloguing archived material

Artist Relations *Bag on Your Head Records, London*
February 1998 to April 2000
Responsible for producing artist schedules i.e. TV, radio, booking hotels and flights etc
Event management and venue sourcing for artists
Liaising with TV and radio pluggers in order to produce artist promotion schedule
Managed ticket requests including festivals and award events
Invoicing, raising purchase orders, and organising artists transport/ couriers

Label Assistant (Work Experience Placement) *Aalto Records, London*
February 1995 to May 1998
Finding and booking venues for band tours negotiating band payment, support acts,
and stage times.
Responsible for listening & reviewing artists demos
Point of contact for label enquiries
Produced promotional singles for distribution to media outlets

Figure 5.03. A chronological résumé.

Chronological résumés are the most common form of résumé I see and, for the live music industry, the most inappropriate. Let me explain.

Your résumé is a marketing message just like your web site and mail outs. The information it contains needs to be relevant and concise. For example, your music industry client does not need to know about the four months you spent working in a coffee house or that you studied marketing at college. Instead you should highlight only the training, experience and an aspiration relevant to the client's needs – finding suitable tour crew.

Chronological résumés are especially problematic when you are just starting out and do not have that many tours or shows to list. Listing every day job and part time position you have held may show you are a diligent worker but shows your client nothing that will convince her you have the skills and experience to solve her problem, which is finding experienced show crew for her tour or event.

Functional résumé

A functional résumé, such as the one shown in figure 5.04, will highlight your suitability to a client, and this is the type you should send.

The functional résumé works for you as it only lists the relevant parts of your work history to date. And if you don't have a relevant work history then the functional résumé will still show a potential client that you are focused and willing to learn.

The 'Job objective' section is the place to state that you are inexperienced in this area but are willing to learn. 'To secure an entry-level stage hand position on domestic and international tours' is an example of a good job objective. It shows you are realistic about your experiences ('level-entry') and the scope of your work ('domestic and international').

Rhoda Managere

Flat 4 Duchess Street, London, ES1 999
Mobile: +44 (0)776 68 • e-mail: rhodmanager@aol.com

Job Objective.
To become an internationally recognised tour and production manager in the live music industry.

Qualifications

- Tour manager responsible for advancing all aspects of a tour (both national and international) including transport, accommodation, budgeting, hiring personnel, creating schedules, technical requirements of sound, lights and staging for performers including Millions Of Americans and First Name Last Name.

- Tour production responsible for advancing all aspects of a tour production including transport, budgeting, hiring personnel, creating schedules, technical requirements of sound, lights and staging for performers including Millions Of Americans and First Name Last Name.

- Company manager responsible for setting up and running tours.

Professional Skills

- Technical skills include sound engineering (CVE), lighting design and backline technician.

- Full UK and European driving licence

- National Rigging Certificate

- MS Office

Education
1979   BA hons English and Drama, London University
1976   3 A-Levels English, Economics and Geography
1974   7 O-Levels including Maths and English

Personal
Date of Birth: 11th November 1957   Nationality: British

Figure 5.04. A functional résumé.

Working on recommendation

A well prepared functional résumé, informative web site, social media interaction and brochures are a good way of responding to a prospective clients request for information. But how do you get to those prospective clients? What does a modern band look for when selecting crew?

I questioned my clients in order to find out how artist managers and booking agents find and hire the crew for their tours and events. I asked each of them a simple question: "How do you choose your Tour Managers and touring crew?"

It turns out 92 % of music industry professionals hire their crew through recommendation from a trusted colleague [14]. It's simple: To get the work you need to be recommended. I will say that again:

To get the work you *need* to be recommended.

Forget about sending unsolicited résumés, bulk email mailings and using web-based 'crew sites' - the top business people in the modern live music industry work from direct contact or recommendation. In fact, the live music business uses it's 'suppliers' just like anyone else uses an electrician or plumber.

For example, I for one do not go around all day thinking about a list of potential plumbers I can call upon if I need to. Rather, I will find myself suddenly needing a plumber and so either: 1) look in Yellow Pages or better still, 2) call someone I know who has used a plumber recently and ask for a recommendation. My experience with live music industry professionals is that they think in the same way about the tour crew they need.

Although booking agents and managers plan tours and concerts for a living, the actual provision and selection of crew, especially tour managers, comes as almost an afterthought. The priority of the manager and booking agent is to get the band on tour, adverts in the press, sponsorship deals in place and the tour funds sorted out.

Working with my clients over the years has led me to the conclusion that you, as a potential/experienced touring professional, should view yourself as one of the plumbers of the tour planning world.

Record companies and booking agents are not employment agencies for touring crew. Your potential clients do not sit around all day planning how to utilise the numerous crew (including you) who have sent in résumés and emails. Ms. Agent will instead probably say to herself: "Well that's the tour planned; the band leave in eight weeks. Oh, better get a Tour Manager and a Front-Of-House engineer I suppose." She will then look around her office and say "Does anyone know a good TM?"

It does not matter how keen you are or how much experience you have; you need to have a previous or current client singing your praises and passing along the word about your skills. Indeed, one of my clients singles out the fact that this very lack of recommendation creates a barrier for prospective TM's and crew [See appendix 2].

Getting those recommendations

So, we have established that you need referrals and recommendations to get employed on a tour or event. And, as with your initial business plan, you should adopt a strategy to contact industry professionals. The following tips may help you to get those referrals.

1. Do not send out emails or letters to managers, agents, record companies or bands if you have had no previous relationship with them.

If you are going to contact someone 'cold' (i.e. you have no previous dealings with them) at least call them on the phone. The advent of email means it is easy for anyone to send off 20 or so emails and then sit back, waiting for the recipients to take action. While not actually spam, this kind of work-seeking email is just as annoying as receiving a 'buy cheap Viagra' email for any music industry professional, so don't do it. At the same time, making a cold phone call is an uncomfortable and nerve-racking process for many of us. However it shows more commitment, and a desire, to make a situation happen. Many music professionals, me included, appreciate the effort of a phone call. Yes, we may be busy, not be able to take your call or be unable to help you. The fact that you actually made a phone call instead of sending an impersonal email is always more impressive. "We take young kids who can be bothered to phone us up – not email, that's just going through the motions and shows no commitment whatsoever," says Andy Docherty of Ad Lib Audio, a PA rental company [18].

When making an employment related call you should always be brief, polite and ensure some follow up action. Introduce yourself to the potential client, having researched them thoroughly. Ask if you may send a résumé by post or email. Remember, you are a freelancer with your own business but you are still going to have to send out a résumé that details your experience and capabilities.

After asking permission to send your résumé always check with the prospective client that you have the all the correct name and company spellings and then hang up, thanking them for their time.

The résumé you send should always reference when you first made contact i.e. "I called you today (01/02) regarding possible jobs on the xxxx tour. I have pleasure in enclosing some information about myself." Offer to follow up the call again in 2-3 weeks to see if the situation has changed or if there are other opportunities.

2. Do make friends with other crew members and keep in regular contact.

All successful tour crew get offered employment that clashes with existing work. This happens to me all the time; I simply say "Thanks for the offer of the work. I'm sorry I am not available for that period. However, I know this really good person who may be able to help". That person could be you. So keep in touch with your crew buddies - Crewspace is one of the best ways of doing this as it is easy and relevant.

3. Do your research.

Find out who is touring, when and where. Look on promoter and venue websites. Subscribe, or have access to, industry trade magazines such as Audience and Billboard and to websites such as CelebrityAccess.com. Remember that most tours are booked between four and eight months in advance, with tickets going on sale only 2-3 months before the tour goes out. The booking of crew can be done at the very last minute stage (as discussed above) but it does no harm to know well in advance that a tour is happening and make yourself known to the relevant artist manager or tour manager.

4. Do keep in touch with previous clients.

It sounds obvious but, as I explained previously, artist managers and booking agents do not really have your employment welfare at the top of their list of priorities. They will not be thinking constantly about giving you work. In order to make them give you work you need to keep in touch. Make sure you are on their 'radar' and at least appear to be genuinely interested in the career of the band they represent. A reminder email or call every 2-3 months should do the trick. At the very least you might get a copy of the band's new album before it is released in the stores.

5. Do get testimonials and recommendations from satisfied clients.

You have already seen that these recommendations and referrals are what will get you future work; make sure you publicise the work you have done. By all means have a website, brochures and résumé. These are tools that will help you get work but if they do not contain testimonials and referrals from previous clients then the effectiveness of these sales materials will be lost.

As soon as you have finished a tour or event, write to the person who directly employed you and ask them to jot something down for you to use in your resume or on your website. Be polite and, if necessary, write out a rough version of what you would like them to say about you. Always make sure you seek their permission to publicise any comment they may have written without solicitation, if they send you a 'thank you' email for instance.

I tend to seek testimonials and comments from my clients immediately after I have finished a contract. I then post these testimonials on my web site. You can see them here: http://www.tourconcepts.com/clients.htm (figure 5.05). You can do the same - set up a Facebook Page and list the clients (bands, agents and managers) you have worked for. Get those testimonials on there!

Remember we all are increasingly time-short and information hungry. A prospective client needs to know you are capable and that you have experience. You are far more likely to get work if your prospective client can check you out by simply going to a web page and getting all the information about you she needs.

Figure 5.05. A page from www.tourconcepts.com showing client testimonials.

6 How do you keep working in the live music business?

Having gained a foothold in the live music business you will need to work extremely hard to then find further employment. You and your new crew business must differentiate itself from the other industry professionals out there. The number of touring professionals out there is fairly small (some estimates put the number as low as 300 touring crew in the UK) and so competition for any employment is fierce.

Following the strategies outlined in chapter 5, 'Getting Hired', will help your business get referrals and more work. I thoroughly recommend you adopt these strategies.

Success will come, in small steps at first, slowly growing your business. As you grow and expand, taking on ever longer and more lucrative tours, it pays to keep your eye on the day-to-day operations of your business. Remember I talked about cash flow in chapter 3, 'Set up your own freelance business'? Well I'm going to expand on this subject here as it is vital to the success of any freelance crew business.

Payment and invoicing

Before you accept any freelance work, you should always check out the financial position of a new client. You may be offered a road crew job by a booking agent, artist manager, or business manager. However, these people do not actually pay your invoice. In nearly all cases, your salary as road crew is paid by the band, either from their own vast cash reserves (if they are U2 or the Dave Matthews Band) or, more likely, from record company tour support. I mention this because it is very easy for an artist manager to call a freelance touring crew person, order that person's services, and then not pay the crew person.

In my experience, as a band becomes successful, they become less responsible for actually finding and hiring their own crew. Hiring is usually done by the artist's management or the band's tour manager. (Booking agents may also be asked to hire crew for their acts although this is not so common).

As a freelancer you are free to choose when you work and for whom. Yes, you have to search for the work, but if you adopt the strategies I have outlined in the previous chapter you should find more than enough clients to give you work.

All the touring crew people I know go through periods of incredible abundance with plenty of work, hot leads, and money rolling in. And then, for whatever reason, there is no work.

A tour can get cancelled, for instance. Or perhaps it is a quiet time of the year, and there simply isn't any work. Even worse you could then be paid late (or not at all) by your client. No current tour work and no income can leave you facing financial ruin.

In order to keep your cash flow healthy and your bank manager happy you need to make sure your invoices are paid. This may be difficult at first. The most important thing to ask a new client is: who is paying me?

Check your client.

Find out who actually will be employing you and who does the hiring. Tour crew usually work directly for the band i.e. they are paid by the band out of the funds available for the tour. In the early stages of the band's career the crew will be friends or people the band know from their home town.

So, the first, and most important, step you should take when offered employment on a tour or show is to find out whom exactly is paying you. Ask the person who calls or hires you as to where your invoice should be sent. Get written invoicing details before you actually go out to work. This may take the form of "Xxx artist care of Xxx business manager" or "Xxx record label." Many bands set up a small company to administer the finances of their touring (usually an LLC or LLP, see chapter 3), in which case your invoice should be sent there. In other cases, all invoicing may be handled by the artist's record company.

When you have found out the invoicing details, you should find a real, live person in the relevant management or record company accounting/accounts payable office. Call that person (don't email them as they can/will ignore your message) to let him or her know who you are and what your role is, and tell that person to expect an invoice from you. Ask whether you need a purchase order[1] number or other reference. Large organizations do not accept invoices for purchases that have not been authorized. Many record companies I work for also require you to be on their supplier list before they will accept an invoice from you. You will therefore have to fill out some forms and return them, a process that can take two to four weeks. Only then can you submit an invoice. Please remember this fact. It can take 4-6 weeks for the necessary paperwork to be completed. You will not get paid until that process is complete. This can have a massive effect on your cash flow.

Get a contract

Draw up a contract. Insist on at least one third of your salary for the road crew work on the tour in advance. Getting a portion of the money up front will help your cash flow and shows commitment from the artist's business team. Likewise, if the tour is going to last for three months or more, then insist on being paid weekly or monthly for the duration of the tour. Can you really afford to work for three months without any income form the tour and then have to wait another thirty days once the tour has finished to get paid? Again, it's all about cash flow. You may be on tour but your rent/mortgage/bills still need to be paid. As I mentioned in chapter 3, many US business management companies will set you up on the artist companies payroll, ensuring weekly salary payments into your account.

---

1   A purchase order is issued by large companies to authorize supply of good and services. You invoice has to tie in with a PO number; otherwise you will not get paid.

Finally, any terms you have for payment should be clearly stated in your contract for road crew work.

The Production Services Association has produced a very useful contract for freelance crew. Although the PSA is based in the UK, the style of the contract is applicable to any freelance technician. Figure 6.01 shows the contract; you can download a free copy of the contract from http://www.livemusicbusiness.com/crew-resources/ tools

THIS AGREEMENT is made the \<date\> day of \<month & year\>

BETWEEN

xxxxxx of 123 xxx xxxxx xxxxx xxxxx. (The Supplier)

AND

(The Client)

CONTRACT DETAILS   **CONTRACT NO.:**

EVENT, PRODUCTION OR TOUR:

DURATION OF THE AGREEMENT: From: **To:**

1.   The Supplier agrees to supply goods/services in accordance with the Schedule attached hereto or as subsequently agreed in writing by the parties hereto.

2.   It is hereby agreed that prior to the signing hereof The Client has had ample opportunity to examine The Supplier's Terms of Business attached hereto and shall be deemed to have unequivocally accepted them.

3.   The total contract price shall be

4.   The terms of payment are

5.   In the event of cancellation of this Agreement by The Client and without prejudice to any rights hereunder or under the Terms of Business attached hereto, The Client will indemnify The Supplier as a result of such cancellation for <   >% of the contract price. Interest at a rate of <   >% per month is liable to be charged on any outstanding balances.

6.   It is a fundamental term of this agreement that the stipulations as to payment contained be fully adhered to by The Client (including an absolute requirement of payment to be made within the times stipulated but subject to the proviso contained in Condition 4) and if for any reason The Client shall be in breach of such stipulations The Supplier shall have the right at its absolute and sole discretion and without prejudice to its other rights hereunder forthwith and without notice to dismantle or remove or otherwise bring to an end any works service goods or other things supplied by The Supplier hereunder and to terminate forthwith this agreement and be under no further liability hereunder to provide any of the services or goods herein agreed.

Signed for and on behalf of   )

The Supplier   )

Date

Signed for and on behalf of   )

The Client   )

Date

IN ADDITION TO SIGNING THE AGREEMENT, THE CLIENT IS REQUESTED TO INITIAL ALL PAGES OF THIS AGREEMENT, THE TERMS OF BUSINESS AND SCHEDULES, AT THE TOP RIGHT HAND CORNER.

TERMS OF BUSINESS:

1.   All services and goods supplied by The Supplier are subject to the terms set out herein and in the Agreement attached unless varied in writing by the parties. The signing of the Agreement shall be deemed to be acceptance of these Terms of Business.

2.   All works goods and services shall be supplied by The Supplier to a good and workman like standard in accordance with the Schedule that is annexed hereto so far as the circumstances shall reasonably allow. The Client shall ensure that the Schedule complies in all respects with their requirements or any authority or any other person or entity involved. The Supplier reserves the rights to alter or amend the Schedule at any time if in the absolute discretion of The Supplier the needs of safety so require.

3.   The Client must ensure that all necessary licenses, consents and authorities to stage the event/s have been obtained and shall indemnify The Supplier in respect of any liability costs or claims arising there from.

4.   The contract price shall be paid strictly in accordance with the terms of payment contained in the Agreement.

5.   The Client shall for the duration of The Agreement place in public liability insurance to a minimum indemnity of £. And shall produce evidence of such insurance at the request of the Supplier.

6.   The Supplier shall for the duration of The Agreement place in public liability insurance to a minimum indemnity of £. And shall produce evidence of such insurance at the request of the Client.

7.   Unless listed in The Suppliers Terms and Conditions, The Client shall be responsible for supplying the items or services listed in the Schedules attached hereto at no cost to The Supplier.

8.   The Client shall ensure that all equipment provided by The Supplier is fully protected from and insured against all risks (including but not limited

to, theft and malicious acts in respect to equipment) and shall produce evidence of such insurance with The Supplier's interest noted thereon at the request of The Supplier.

9.   The Supplier shall not be liable in respect of any damage caused to the site(s) or venue(s) either during the event/s or as a result of the erection and/or dismantling of equipment and services unless such damage results from the negligent act or admission of The Supplier, the servants, agents or sub-contractors, or persons for whom they are responsible.

10.   The Supplier shall so far as is reasonably practicable follow the Health and Safety rules and arrangements as set out in The Client's Health and Safety Policy.

11.   Unless otherwise agreed in writing by both parties to this Agreement, The Supplier acknowledges and accepts that:

The Client will not be providing First Aid cover for The Supplier or For The Suppliers employees for the duration of the Agreement

The Supplier will be responsible for making First Aid arrangements according to the standards set by Health and Safety (First Aid) Regulations 1981 for The Supplier and for The Suppliers employees.

12.   The Supplier shall keep secret and shall not use or disclose and shall use his/her best endeavours to prevent the use or disclosure by or to any person any of The Client's or The Client's clients confidential information which came to his/her knowledge during the engagement. The restriction shall apply during the Suppliers engagement without any time limit but shall cease to apply to information or knowledge which the Supplier establishes has in it's entirety become public knowledge otherwise than through the unauthorised disclosure or other breach to The Suppliers part of that restriction. Confidential information means all confidential information relating to the organisation, finances, business activities and private activities of

The Client, The Client's client and either of their
employees and agents, suppliers or advisors. The Supplier further agrees not to use any of the information
gleaned during the term of this Agreement to directly
or indirectly solicit business from any of the Client's clients.

13.   The Supplier shall not be liable for any breach
of the Agreement or terms hereof where such a breach
was caused by or substantially contributed to by any
cause beyond the control of the Supplier including
(without limitation) Act of God insurrections riot
civil commotion's Government or any other enforce-
able regulations embargoes explosions strikes labour
disputes fire and exceptionally adverse weather. The
Supplier's Sub-contractors shall be deemed to be parties to The Agreement for the purpose of obtaining
the protection of this clause and the Client shall
indemnify the Supplier in respect to any claim by a
third party in respect of which liability is excluded
by this clause provided always that the Supplier shall
use it's best endeavours to prevent such a breach or
mitigate the effects thereof.

14.   The Client shall make any assignment for the
benefit of its creditors, commit and/or fail to inform
The Supplier of any act of bankruptcy or if, being a
limited company, shall suffer any receiver of it's
assets to be appointed or upon commencement of any
winding up or upon failure to pay any sum due to The
Supplier whether due under this contract or otherwise
upon other breach of contract by the Client, The Supplier shall be entitled to cease work immediately and
to dismantle remove or otherwise bring to and end any
works service goods or other things supplied by The
Supplier hereunder. Upon ceasing work dismantling,
removing or otherwise bringing to and end any works
service goods or other things supplied by The Supplier
hereunder, this contract shall be deemed to have been
terminated but without affecting any pre-existing
rights of the parties including the Supplier's right
to receive payment of the full price of the contract
without deduction.

15.   Any contract to which these terms apply shall be in accordance with the laws of England and the parties agree to accept the jurisdiction of the courts of England.

SCHEDULES

The Supplier will provide for the duration of The
Agreement:

The Client will provide for the duration of the Agreement:

*Figure 6.01. A contract between freelancer and the client agreeing to supply
good and services. It is not an employment contract. For more information
see www.psa.org.uk (Courtesy of the PSA)*

Pay rates

Economics in general, and that of the touring market, have not really supported an increase in pay amounts to tour crew in the last 20 years. There is no automatic monthly pay check plopping into your bank account when you freelance - you need to work in order to get paid. So say you have just finished a two-month arena tour with an international superstar. You may have been paid pretty well and you may be doing okay financially. However, that money is not going to last forever and you are going to have to go back to work at some point. What if your next job is with four kids in a van - playing bars? You cannot charge those kids (or their management) arena-tour rates, despite the years of skill and experience you have built up. It does not matter who you have worked for and how long you have been touring - you cannot simply set a fee and expect to get it.

So what do you do? Well, there is no international standard pay scale for touring road crew. My tour crew survey [14] shows that the majority of crew earn $US 151-200, £151-200 or $AUS 101- 150 a day (figure 6.02). You charge what you think you are worth, but is that a realistic approach? (I think I am worth my weight in gold, but I cannot realistically charge that for a tour. At the time of writing, gold is $56,000 per kilo. I weigh 71 kilos—you do the math).

You could pluck a figure out of the air and present that to the band as your fee. I would not advise this though. If you are challenged by a prospective employer about your proposed fees, you need some formula that you can use to explain how you arrived at the daily rate. A good starting point is to take the minimum wage for your state or country, multiply it by 10 (for the average 10 hours a day you work), and then add an extra amount that you feel is appropriate, depending on your skills and experience.

Suppose you live in California and you have been hired by a band that you have previously worked with, but who have just been signed to a record company. They used to pay you $50 a day with no per diems and no wage for days off. You want to take things to a more professional level with them, so you ask for $110 and a $15 per diem for days off. They balk at your request until you explain your reasoning:

Minimum wage in the state of California is $8.00 an hour at the time of this writing. You work an average of 10 hours a day, so $8.00 x 10 = $80. Add another $30 for the skills and experience you can bring to them, and this gets you $110 per day. You then explain that you do not really need a per diem on show days because there will be food and drink provided by the promoters. However, you would like $15 per diem on the days off because there will be no supplied catering and you will have to fend for yourself.

The band can either accept your offer or not; the point is that they can see the reasoning and that you are not simply doubling your fees because they now have a record company backing them.

How much are prepared to pay a Tour Manager PER DAY for a club tour
(250-1000 capacity venues)?.

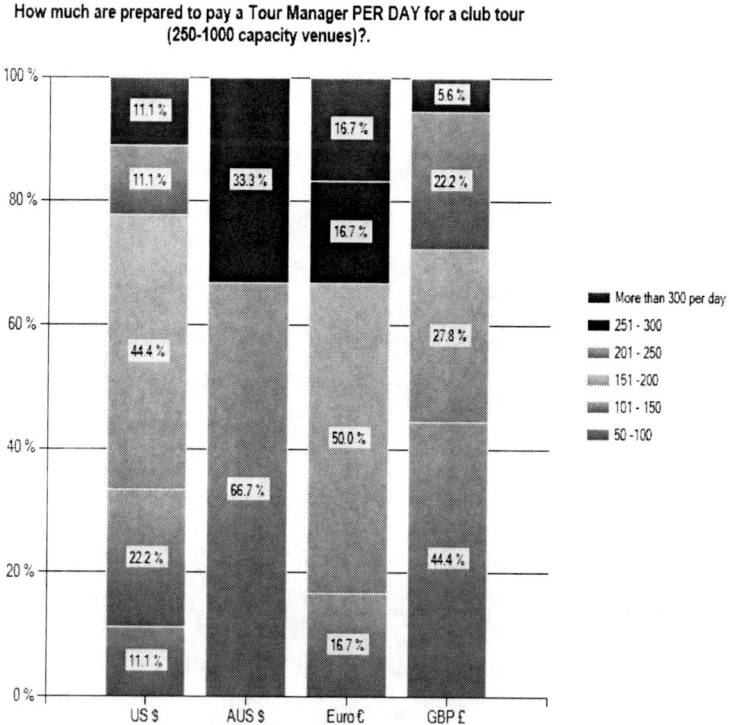

Figure 6.02. The amount live music business professionals are prepared to pay touring crew at club level. (Image from 'Concert Tour management Survey 2010).

Plan ahead

As soon as you commence a tour, start to plan your next period of work. Make sure you have your marketing materials (résumés, business cards and web sites) updated and available to people you may meet on the current tour.

Why, well imagine that you finish a tour at the end of March. You know that tours and events are booked at least 3 months in advance. It will not be easy to go out and get another tour straight away. It may take you a couple of weeks to find and be hired onto another tour (if you can be hired at all). The new tour then may then not be going out for another 1-2 months. You are therefore looking at 2 to 5 months without work. Will the pay check from your last tour last that long?

Health and conditions

If you like comfort, regular food, lots of sleep, a modicum of privacy, and job security, then touring life is definitely not for you. Sleeper bus tours are especially hard on the more sensitive people (figure 6.03). I always liken touring on a sleeper bus to being in a travelling student or frat house—mess, noise, unsociable behaviour, and more people than there should be, all packed into a small space. There is no privacy on a tour bus, a fact that seriously irritates and upsets many people. I am serious—this is not a glamorous life.

Your health may also suffer. A combination of lack of proper sleep; moving from hot, sweaty rooms to the cold outside; lack of decent food; heavy lifting; and too much drinking and partying will soon take its toll. At the very least, you will get a bad cold—a cold that will spread around the tour bus in no time.

You can help yourself to avoid getting sick but this means you are going to have to make a great deal of adjustments. Learn to live and function without much sleep for instance. It may seem harsh, but your body will adjust. You cannot allow yourself to get cranky because you have not slept—no one sleeps properly on tour.

This is how I survive touring:

- Make sure you learn how to nap—sleep anytime you possibly can.

- Buy earplugs and eyeshades to enable you to sleep anywhere.

- Make sure your cell phone has the loudest alarm known to man.

- Get a backup alarm as well.

- Never rely on hotel wake up calls.

- Drink plenty of water all day.

- Ask the tour manager to strike meats and cheeses from the rider deli tray. Meats and cheeses go off pretty quickly in a warm dressing room. This can cause food poisoning.

- Don't store any food in the bus fridge. Food left in a tour bus fridge tends to stay in there for a long time because no-one is responsible enough to tidy up the fridge. Eventually this old food will go mouldy. Mould can contaminate other food, again causing food poisoning.

Finally, this job is murder on relationships. Friends, family, and significant others get resentful of the amount of time that you are away. The worst part is when you promise to call, and some disaster takes place on the tour, and you end up being super busy when you should be calling home. This does not go over well. Work hard at keeping your communications current—an e-mail, Skype call, facebook message, or text once or twice a day will keep you in people's heart and minds.

As Andy Dimmack, backline technician for Pavement Franz Ferdinand and Super Furry Animals, says, "The worst thing about being on tour? Being away from family and loved ones." [19]

Figure 6.03. The sleeper coach. Your home for a very long time. I hope you like it.

7 Conclusion

I f you have followed the steps and advice contained in this book you should be in a good position to follow your dream and continue your career in the live music industry. I want to leave you with a final check list of actions[1], inspiration and motivational thoughts in order to fill you with energy and excitement for the road ahead (pun intended.)

1. Have a solid résumé. You are starting a business and may never need it, but refining and improving your resume helps you to define your skills.

2. Prepare yourself mentally and spiritually to face rejection. Entering a new career and establishing a new business is not going to be easy, especially in tough economic times.

3. Use your network. When things get tough you can turn to your network for help, guidance or reassurance.

4. Set short-, medium- and long-term goals and keep measuring your progress towards those goals. Your freelance tour crew business may not be successful for a while and you can take comfort in the satisfaction of reaching steps

---

1   Adapted from 'How to get A Job In The Music Industry', Hatscheck,K. Berklee

along the way.

5. Learn to ask intelligent questions. You need to appear as an asset in client meetings and networking opportunities, not a liability.

6. Do your research and learn as much as you can about the way the live music industry works. Study the top promoters and booking agents to understand the 'supply and demand' of this business.

7. Finally, remember that thousands of people before you have followed their dream and now work as freelance crew on-the-road. You are no different from those people – if they did it, then so can you. Keep a positive attitude and you will succeed!

Appendix 1

Specific job roles, skills and qualifications

The following pages contain a brief list of the roles of the various people involved in creating a modern show or tour. There is no specific crew roster that a tour MUST have; in many cases one person will take have more than role on a tour. However, one attribute common to all these jobs is a passion for live music!

Artist management

The artist manager acts is responsible for overseeing every aspect of the artist's career. This is not a recognised touring position as such but the manager will probably accompany the artist as they start out performing live. The manager will then appoint a tour manager to oversee the concert performances as the artist becomes established, then visiting the tour as it plays in key markets and more important cities.

Level of tour:

Bars to stadiums.

Qualifications or training available:

Yes. Artist management, music management and live event management degrees and training courses available.

Employment status:

Usually self employed. Successful artist managers will then employ full-time junior managers and assistants.

Skills and personality:

- Total understanding of every aspect of the music business – record company deals, publishing deals, synchronisation deals, copyright law, radio & TV promotion, touring, offline and online marketing and branding opportunities.

- Office productivity software skills – Word, Excel, email client.

- Self-motivated.

- Established industry network.

- Good business acumen.

- Calm under pressure.

- Passionate about their artist.

Equipment needed:

Telephone, smart phone (capable of receiving emails on the move), laptop or desktop computer and a reliable internet connection.

Comments:

The manager's income is dependent on the earning potential of her artist: good artist managers will therefore set clear boundaries when it come to responsibilities – spending all day sorting out her clients laundry or ordering taxis is not an effective, or income-realising, use of the mangers time.

Booking agent

Finds paid performance work for the artist. Not a touring position as such.

Level of tour:

Bar to stadium.

Qualifications or training available:

Not specifically. Live events management and music management course may touch on some aspects of becoming an agent. Most agents learn from mentors or from on-the-job training.

Employment status:

Self-employed initially or may join an established company as a junior booking agent.

Skills and personality:

- Total understanding of the live music business – concert promotion, contracts and riders, foreign artist taxation, visas and work permits, ticketing and merchandising. Some knowledge of tour production will also be very useful.

- Office productivity software skills – Word, Excel, email client.

- Must be able to establish and grow a network.

- Equipment needed:

- Telephone, smart phone (capable of receiving emails on the move), laptop or desktop computer, printer and an internet connection.

Comments:

Booking agents have to go to shows 4 or 5 nights a week in order to check out new talent and see existing clients.

Concert promoter

Finds and hires venues, creates advertising and sells tickets for shows and tours. Not a touring position.

Level of tour:

Bar to stadium.

Qualifications or training available:

Yes. Live event management and show promotion courses and degrees available.

Employment status:

Self-employed initially. May join established promoter as junior promoter or assistant.

Skills and personality:

- Total understanding of the live music business – concert promotion, contracts and riders, foreign artist taxation, visas and work permits, ticketing and merchandising. Some knowledge of tour production will also be very useful.

- Office productivity software skills – Word, Excel, email client.

- Talent spotting skills.

- Good financial acumen.

- Equipment needed:

- Telephone, laptop or desktop computer and an internet connection.

Comments:

Promoting is a financially risky occupation. Competing events, the weather and transport problems can all affect the amount of people who turn up at a show. A successful promoter must promote as many events as possible and be ruthless in cutting costs – which sometimes is to the detriment of the artist and audience.

Promoter's rep

Represents the promoter at each show. A rep will probably travel with the band and crew if a string of dates is being promoted by one particular promoter. In any case, promoter's reps have to travel to each show they are working on.

Level of tour:

300 capacities and upwards.

Qualifications or training available:

None that is specific to this role. Live music management or events management courses may be useful.

Employment status:

Freelance.

Skills and personality:

- Total understanding of the live music business – concert promotion, contracts and riders and foreign artist taxation.

- Self-motivated.

- Responsible.

- Excellent financial skills – show settlements, taxation etc.

- Show production knowledge is very useful.

- Office productivity software skills – Word, Excel, email client.

Equipment needed:

Telephone, laptop. a device capable of sending and receiving emails on the move, portable printer, car.

Comments:

A promoter's rep has a great deal of responsibility as they not only have to make sure the show runs smoothly, they also have to take of the payment to the artist and make sure that the promoter receives every penny left from ticket sales. Working as a rep is great way to see all sides of modern touring – reps often move into tour management.

Tour manager

The tour manager does not book the shows but is responsible for all aspects of the panning and logistics of the tour. Travels with the band and oversees the day-to-day running of the shows.

Level of tour:

300 capacities and upwards.

Qualifications or training available:

There are no specific concert tour management courses (yet) but degrees and training are available in live event management and music management.

Employment status:

Freelance. The tour manager is usually hired by the artists themselves.

Skills and personality:

- Total understanding of the music business – concert promotion, contracts and riders, foreign artist taxation, visas and work permits, ticketing, merchandising, radio & TV promotion.

- Office productivity software skills – Word, Excel, email client.

- Financial responsibility and training.

- Self motivated

- Excellent people skills.

- Calm under pressure

Equipment needed:

Cell phone, laptop with office productivity software, a device capable of sending and receiving emails on the move, a portable printer, flash light and a bottle opener.

Comments:

Even though the tour manager is expected to have an encyclo-paedic knowledge of concert touring it is probably more important that they know which specialist to ask in case of an issue or challenge.

The tour manager will act as tour accountant on smaller level tours (200 – 5000 capacity venues) – dealing with the payments and show settlements; this role may be taken over by a dedicated tour accountant on larger tours (see below).

Production manager

Responsible for the production elements of large-scale touring: sound, light and video equipment, staging, power and associated transport.

Level of tour:

Any tour carrying its own production, usually of venues with capacities of 2000 plus.

Qualifications or training available:

Yes.

Employment status:

Freelance. Hired directly by the artist via the tour manager.

Skills and personality:

- Complete understanding of the technical requirements of staging a modern music event.

- Employment and 'working-time' regulations

- Health and safety regulations

- Office productivity software – Word, excel, email clients

- Technical design/CAD software

- Good leader

- Stamina

Equipment needed:

Cell phone, laptop with office productivity software, a device capable of sending and receiving emails on the move, a portable printer, flash light, Personal Protective Equipment (hi-vis vest, steel cap boots, hard hat).

Comments:

No-one should underestimate the responsibility of the production manager. There have been a few high-profile accidents involving stage and rigging collapses recently, the responsibility for which lies directly with the production management. Don't put yourself forward for this role if you don't know what you are doing!

Audio crew – systems tech

Set-up and de-rig of sound equipment on a tour carrying its own sound equipment. The system tech is there to help and support the audio engineers that mix the Front-of-House and monitor (stage) sound for the band.

Level of tour:

Production level, usually venues with capacities of 2000 plus.

Qualifications or training available:

Yes. Audio and live audio training and degrees as well as manufacture specific training i.e. L-Acoustics 'Certified V-Dosc Engineer' accreditation or Midas Consoles 'Certified Digital Users' course.

Employment status:

Freelance. Hired by the sound rental company. Manufacturers may also send their research and development (R&D) employees out on the road if supplying new products and technology to a rental company.

Skills and personality:

- Ability to set-up and run pro-audio equipment.

- Work as part of team.

- Equipment needed:

- Personal Protective Equipment (hi-vis vest, steel cap boots, hard hat), flash light, electrical multi-meter, tool kit.

Comments:

There are many specialism's' developing in concert audio such as audio networking and wireless ('RF') audio; anyone who has training and experience in these areas is going to stand a better chance of working permanently. Unfortunately system techs very rarely get to actually mix audio at concerts.

Audio crew – band

To mix the Front-of-House and monitor (stage) sound for the band.

Level of tour:

Bar to stadium.

Qualifications or training available:

Yes. Audio and live audio training and degrees.

Employment status:

Freelance. Hired directly by the band.

Skills and personality:

- Ability to set-up and run pro-audio equipment.

- Mix audio to a consistently high standard.

- Work as part of team

Equipment needed:

Personal Protective Equipment (hi-vis vest, steel cap boots, hard hat), flash light, headphones, electrical multi-meter, tool kit.

Comments:

Most bands will hire a sound man' (audio engineer) before they even consider any other crew. Working with a band from day one may not earn you much money but will give you a chance to grow with an act and (hopefully) share in the success later down the road.

I recommend you go on as many manufacturer-led audio training courses as possible; those guys want to use their gear and you get to play with lots of shiny new toys!

Lighting crew – systems tech

Set-up and de-rig of lighting equipment on a tour carrying its own equipment. The system tech is there to help and support the Lighting Designer and/or operator.

Level of tour:

Production level, usually venues with capacities of 2000 plus.

Qualifications or training available:

Yes. Lighting design and technology training and degrees as well as manufacture specific courses.

Employment status:

Freelance, hired by the lighting rental company. Manufacturers may also send their research and development (R&D) employees out on the road if supplying new products and technology to a rental company.

Skills and personality:

- Ability to set-up and run pro-lighting equipment.

- Work at heights.

- Work as part of team

- Proficiency in lighting design software, (WYSIWYG etc) is an advantage.

Equipment needed:

Personal Protective Equipment (fall-arrest harness, hi-vis vest, steel cap boots, hard hat), flash light, electrical multi-meter, tool kit.

Comments:

Lighting technology is advancing at an alarming rate as the world looks to LED and other non-tungsten technology. Make sure you subscribe to all the relevant trade magazines and get on as many manufacturer-led training courses as possible in order to keep your knowledge current.

Lighting crew – Lighting Designer/operator

The lighting designer ('LD') creates the look and feel for the stage lighting, indicating which lamps and fixtures should go where. In the case of a small club show this design takes place in the afternoon of the show and at production level will programmed in a pre-production rehearsal some weeks in advance. The LD may then operate the show on tour or designate an operator to 'run' the various scene changes.

Level of tour:

Bar to stadium.

Qualifications or training available:

Yes. Lighting for music events courses and manufacturer-lead training available.

Employment status:

Freelance, hired directly by the band.

Skills and personality:

- Ability to design and operate a professional lighting show.

- Be confident and competent with emerging lighting control technologies.

- Work as part of a team.

- Work at heights.

Equipment needed:

Personal Protective Equipment (fall-arrest harness, hi-vis vest, steel cap boots, hard hat), flash light, electrical multi-meter, tool kit. Lighting design software and a powerful computer would be an advantage.

Comments:

Increasing integration of traditional lighting and new video technology means the modern LD needs to really keep herself up-to-date with emerging technology. Subscription to relevant trade magazines and attendance at trade shows such as PLASA and NAMM is a must.

Video crew

Set-up, operation and de-rig of the video elements of a modern concert. This includes video screens to enhance visibility for the audience of the artist on-stage as well as video-as-lighting effects. The video crew includes screen technicians, projection technicians, vision mix operators; graphics mix operators and camera people.

Level of tour:

Production level, usually venues with capacities of 2000 plus.

Qualifications or training available:

Yes. Video and lighting for music events courses and manufacturer-lead training available.

Employment status:

Freelance, hired by the video equipment rental company. Manufacturers may also send their research and development (R&D) employees out on the road if supplying new products and technology to a rental company.

Skills and personality:

- Ability to set-up and run pro-video projection, graphics and camera equipment.

- Work at heights.

- Work as part of team

- Proficiency in media server software an advantage.

Equipment needed:

Personal Protective Equipment (fall-arrest harness, hi-vis vest, steel cap boots, hard hat), flash light, electrical multi-meter, tool kit.

Comments:

Video is ubiquitous in modern concert touring. Lighting designers and operators are best placed to make the transition to this medium as they (should) understand colour theory and the craft of stage lighting. There is a bewildering range of technologies and disciplines in this one area however. You have to understand screen technology, LED devices, front and rear projection, media servers, and vision mixers as well as camera operation. Training is essential.

Backline crew

Set-up, maintenance and pack down of the artist's instruments – drums, bass, guitars, keyboards, stage computers etc, as well as the supervision of the artists stage environment – towels, water and set lists.

Level of tour:

Bar to stadium.

Qualifications or training available:

No specific 'backline technician' courses but you could study electrical engineering for musical and consumer devices. You should also be qualified or have extensive experience of relevant software programs (Pro Tools for instance).

Employment status:

Freelance. You will be hired by the band.

Skills and personality:

- Understanding of how a gig 'works'.

- Encyclopaedic knowledge of musical instruments.

- Electrical safety.

- Knowledge of wireless ('RF') transmission for instruments.

- Work as part of team.

- Excellent people skills.

- Calm under pressure.

- Ability to fault-find and solve problems.

Equipment needed:

Personal Protective Equipment (hi-vis vest, steel cap boots, hard hat), flash light, electrical multi-meter, tool kit and a workbox with relevant test gear for your specialism.

Comments:

You will have a close working relationship with the bands you work for as a backline tech. You, as opposed to any other crew member, will be seen by the audience on the same stage as their idols. Don't let that go your head though; you are not part of the band and you are there to do YOUR job.

Rigger

To help the sound, lighting and video system crews to 'fly' their equipment above the stage. The rigger will go into the roof of the venue to create 'points' from which steel cables and lifting motors can be attached; these are used to lift the lighting and video trusses into the air.

Level of tour:

Any tour carrying its own production, usually of venues with capacities of 2000 plus.

Qualifications or training available:

Yes. There is increasing regulation in this area – any serious rigger should make sure they are qualified or union-assessed as to their competence.

Employment status:

Freelance.

Skills and personality:

- Head for heights!

- Awareness of health and safety regulations.

- Understanding of safe working weight load limits for venue structures, motors, cables, shackles and harnesses.

Equipment needed:

Personal Protective Equipment (Fall-arrest harness, hi-vis vest, steel cap boots, hard hat).

Comments:

Riggers have an enormous responsibility placed upon them these days. More rigging points and increased load-bearing components are required for shows with more staging, more video and more lighting elements. These productions still have to load in and be set up in the same time however; this places increasing pressure on riggers to get the points put in and the equipment flown safely.

Caterer

Cooks hot, tasty food for appreciative road crew and unappreciative artists every day of the tour.

Level of tour:

Any tour carrying its own production (not USA), plus festivals.

Qualifications or training available:

Yes but not specifically for on-tour catering. You should have first hand-experience of working in a very busy kitchen with very demanding customers.

Employment status:

Freelance, hired by the tour catering company. May be employed full-time in the USA by a company supplying catering services to a venue.

Skills and personality:

- Good cook

- Excellent people skills

- Ability to improvise

- Stamina

Equipment needed:

Tour caterers travel with ovens, refrigerators, pots and pans, flatware and cutlery provided by the on-tour catering company. You would want your own aprons, hat and specialised knives though.

Comments:

There are not many opportunities for touring as a chef in the US as many venues have existing contracts with companies that provide food and beverage to the public as well as to the visiting artist and crew.

This is not the case in Europe or Australia; however tour caterers have being the distinction of being 'first in, last out' at any show – it is NOT a glamorous life.

Stagehand

Assists with the load-in, set up and load-out of a modern concert.

Level of tour:

Bar to stadium.

Qualifications or training available:

There are some stage management and production courses. Any technical (lighting, sound etc) course will also be useful. Look at ways to expand your specialism; fork lift, Manitou operation and rigging training for instance.

Employment status:

Freelance.

Skills and personality:

- Work as part of team.

- Follow directions.

- Good time keeping.

- Willingness to learn.

- Work at heights.

- Stamina.

- Physical strength.

Equipment needed:

Personal Protective Equipment (hi-vis vest, steel cap boots, hard hat), adjustable spanner and a flash light.

Comments:

Being a stagehand is about as unglamorous as it gets. You will be working 12-16 hour days with little thanks. It is also the best way to observe how a modern concert 'works' and to meet existing touring crew first hand.

Driver

Driving of vans, trucks or tour buses.

Level of tour:

Vans – bar to stadium. Trucks and buses are usually found on tours carrying their own production elements i.e. in venues with a capacity of 2000 or more.

Employment status:

Freelance. You will be hired by the trucking or bussing company supplying the tour.

Skills and personality:

- Valid driving licence, no endorsements or penalty points.

- Appropriate licence for driving private, public or freight transport.

- Excellent people skills.

- Ability to work as part of team.

- Understand tour merchandise operations (see 'Comments' below)

- Ability to operate a spotlight (see 'Comments' below)

Equipment needed:

The tour transportation will usually supply the bus or truck. Some owner/operators will have their own bus or truck.

Comments:

Bus and truck drivers can make extra money on tour by helping to sell merchandise or operating spotlights as part of the lighting crew.

Tour security

To provide security and close protection services to the touring artist as well as advice for the safety of the entire touring party.

Level of tour:

Whenever the artist or artist's management deem it to be necessary or perceive a threat.

Qualifications or training available:

Yes. Courses in crowd management, event security and close protection are available. Many countries now require security operatives, at whatever level, to be licensed. You should enquire as to the relevant licensing where you live.

Employment status:

Freelance or maybe self-employed running your own security company.

Skills and personality:

- Relevant close protection, crowd management and crowd safety training.

- Excellent people skills.

- Self motivation.

- Stamina.

Merchandiser

To sell t-shirts, CDs, buttons, posters and other tour memorabilia at concerts.

Level of tour:

Bar to mid-level production (venues of 5000 capacity).

Qualifications or training available:

None.

Employment status:

Freelance.

Skills and personality:

- Excellent people skills.

- Excellent financial skills.

- Office productivity software skills – Word, Excel, email client.

- Good organisational skills.

- Willingness to learn.

- Aesthetic sense – able to create an inviting display of merchandise.

- Financially responsible.

Equipment needed:

Personal Protective Equipment (hi-vis vest, steel cap boots, hard hat), flash light, cash box, Sharpies, laptop computer to capture email addresses.

Comments:

The individual tour merchandiser becomes irrelevant at venues above capacities of 5000 or more. At that level the job of selling the bands merchandise is usually grabbed by the venue itself (for a percentage of the gross takings) or contracted out to a merchandising company. However selling merch for a small to intermediate level band is still the best way to get to know the live music business and establish a network of touring contacts – just make sure you make yourself useful to the rest of the touring crew before the doors open.

Tour accountant

To oversee the collection and payment of all tour-related monies.

Level of tour:

Larger production tours of venues with capacities of 10,000 plus.

Qualifications or training available:

There are no specific tour-related accountancy courses and you would have to have passed a relevant accountancy degree to be taken seriously.

Employment status:

Freelance or full-time as part of the artist's management company.

Skills and personality:

- Total understanding of the live music business –contracts and riders, foreign artist taxation, visas and work permits, ticketing and merchandising. Some knowledge of tour production will also be very useful.

- A financial accountancy degree or award.

Equipment needed:

Cell phone, laptop with office productivity software and a portable printer.

Stylist - Wardrobe

Role:

To oversee the preparation and upkeep of stage clothes and costumes for the artist and other touring musicians, dancers and performers.

Level of tour:

Larger production tours of venues with capacities of 5,000 plus.

Qualifications or training available:

Yes but none specific to concert touring. Theatre costume design degrees will give you the necessary knowledge of stage clothing, quick changing etc.

Employment status:

Freelance.

Skills and personality:

Costume design and upkeep in a theatre/concert environment.

Excellent people skills

Ability to work as part of team

Work under pressure

Equipment needed:

Equipment for haberdashery and millinery repairs, cell phone, laptop with office productivity software and a portable printer.

Appendix 2
Quotes from live music business professionals.

These are extracts from the interviews I conducted with various music industry proffesionals.

Getting started:

"I didn't do any formal training to become a Tour Manager it was all on the job training (in other words you learn how to do it or it doesn't get done). No one taught me or gave any lessons and the same goes for engineering. The best knowledge I gained was, and still is, always from other TM's and engineers experience and experiences. When you hear that someone has messed up royally you feel bad for them but you also make a mental note not to do the same thing. Talking to people who do the job is invaluable and will teach you a lot."

-Timm Cleasby. Tour Manager - The Artic Monkeys, Last Shadows Puppets

"I got started in the job by getting on to the crew in the student union when I was at university. When I graduated I got in with a small PA company & did 3 years with them, followed by a bigger PA company then direct work for bands."

-Craig Donaldson. Monitor engineer. Clients include Tricky, Morcheeba, Blur, The Rapture and Super Furry Animals.

How do you choose your Tour Managers and touring crew?

"By word of mouth - speaking to a band, band manager or agent who recommends someone and I recommend to other people TM's that I have worked with and had a "good experience" with."

- Steve Beckett, Warp Records

"Basically over the years I've got to build up a list of people in that position who I like and trust and would have no problems recommending to my clients when they ask."

-Geoff Meall, The Agency Group

"I use/ recommend anyone that I have work with that is a capable, reliable & trust worthy person."

-Jean Coffey, ATC Management

"We have a number of TM's we work with that we trust and use regularly which we could recommend. Other than that it is simply someone you trust with your money but has the experience to run the tour and handle the budget."

- Richard Smith, Mission Control Artists Agency

"We don't choose at all really we just recommend either having worked with them or them recommended to us by someone we work with. Kind of like a 6 degrees of separation which can be quite hard for tour managers and crew to break into."

-Eileen Mulligan, Primary Talent.

References

1. Sandall, R. The Day the Music Industry Died. The Times Online. [Online] 2007. [Accessed: 25 January 2009.] http://entertainment.timesonline.co.uk/tol/arts_and_entertainment/music/article2602597.ece.

2. Billboard. 2010 in Touring: Tough Times on The Road. Billboard Biz. [Online] December 2010. [Accessed: 11 December 2010.] http://www.billboard.biz/bbbiz/genre/rock-and-pop/2010-in-touring-tough-times-on-the-road-1004134445.story.

3. Hiatt, B. Rock & Roll:Richest Rock Stars 2006 - Tour Giants Dominate Biz. Rolling Stone. 2007, 996.

4. Barth, Chris. U2 Top Rock's Richest List. Rolling Stone. [Online] July 2010. [Accessed: 6 January 2011.] http://www.rollingstone.com/music/news/u2-top-rocks-richest-list-20100716.

5. Audience Magazine. Managing Talent. Live UK. 2007, 94, p. 15.

6. Universal Music Group. Handbook.

7. Passman, Donald S. All You Need to Know About The Music Business. UK Edition. London : Penguin Books, 2002.

8. Live Nation Entertainment. Live Nation Entertainment Investor & Analyst Day. Beverly Hills : Live Nation Entertainment, Inc., 2010.

9. Interview with Anthony Oates.

10. Interview with Dave Rupsch.

11. Interview with John Jackson.

12. Allen, Glen. Playing in the mud. Guardian. [Online] 22 April 2008. [Accessed: 25 January 2009.] http://www.guardian.co.uk/education/2008/apr/22/highereducation.uk4.

13. Interview with Chris Taplin.

14. Tour Concepts. Concert Tour Management Survey 2010. London : Tour Concepts, 2010.

15. Bly, Bob. Selling Your Services. New York : Henry Holt and Company, 1991.

16. Wordpress. Home. Wordpress.org. [Online] 2011. [Accessed: 14 January 2011.] http://
wordpress.org/.

17. Facebook. Statistics. Facebook.com. [Online] January 2011. [Accessed: 14 January 2011.]
http://www.facebook.com/press/info.php?statistics.

18. Education: a bridge not far enough? Lighting & Sound International. 11, Eastbourne :
PLASA Media Ltd, 2010, Vol. 25.

19. Crew Cuts:Andy Dimmack. Lighting & Sound International. 12, Eastbourne : PLASA
Media Ltd, 2010, Vol. 23.

20. Reynolds, Andrew. The Tour Book - How to get Your Music on the Road. Boston :
Cengage Learning, 2007.

21. Reynolds, S., 2012. How Rave Music Conquered America. [Online] Available at: http://
www.guardian.co.uk/music/2012/aug/02/how-rave-music-conquered-america [Accessed
February 2012].

CPSIA information can be obtained
at www.ICGtesting.com
Printed in the USA
FFOW03n2334150116
20528FF